RAIL CENTRES:
CLAPHAM JUNCTION

Above:
No 35019 *French Line C.G.T.* approaches Clapham in May
1961 with the down 'Atlantic Coast Express'; two Maunsell
brake composites make a change from the Bulleid stock
forming the rest of the train. 'A' box on the left and 'B' box
on the right frame the express, surprisingly with no other
train in view. *Ian Allan Library — G.F.Heiron*

RAIL CENTRES:
CLAPHAM JUNCTION
J.N. FAULKNER

B L P

Nottingham

Booklaw Publications

Contents

Right:
The 15.30 Victoria-Gatwick Airport, behind No 73208 *Croydon 1883-1983*, swings away from the South Western main line beyond Clapham Junction on 13 April 1989. *C. J. Marsden*

First published 1991
by Ian Allan Ltd

© J. N. Faulkner, 1991

This edition published 2008 by Booklaw Publications
382, Carlton Hill,
Nottingham NG4 1JA

ISBN 1-901945-27-8

Printed by
The Amadeus Press,
Cleckheaton, West Yorkshire

Preface

To the layman the phrase 'Rail Centre' immediately conjures up the idea of Clapham Junction. Though it was a comparative latecomer on the railway scene, the station's history is described in these pages, together with the development of traffic on the various lines serving 'The Junction', which has led to its present distinction of being Britain's busiest railway station.

I would like to express my thanks to the many people who have contributed information and photographic material or provided facilities for this book, including Denis Cullum, Alan A.Jackson, Colin Marsden, Brian Morrison, Reg Randell, R.F.Roberts, R.E.Ruffell and R.A.Williams, also British Rail Southern Region, the National Railway Museum, the Public Record Office, the Railway Club, Wandsworth Public Libraries and the Ian Allan Library.

J.N.Faulkner
Surbiton, May 1991.

Abbreviations

BEF	British Expeditionary Force	N&SWJR	North & South Western Junction Railway
BoT	Board of Trade	POSB	Post Office Savings Bank
DTp	Department of Transport	RCH	Railway Clearing House
ER	Eastern Region	RR	Richmond Railway
GCR	Great Central Railway	SER	South Eastern Railway
GNR	Great Northern Railway	SECR	South Eastern & Chatham Railway
GWR	Great Western Railway	SR	Southern Railway or Southern Region
KESR	Kent & East Sussex Railway	TPO	Travelling Post Office
L&B	London & Brighton Railway	TVR	Thames Valley Railway
L&S	London & Southampton Railway	VS&PR	Victoria Station & Pimlico Railway
LBSCR	London Brighton & South Coast Railway	VSOE	Venice Simplon Orient Express
LCDR	London Chatham & Dover Railway	WARS	Waterloo Area Resignalling Scheme
LMR	London Midland Region	WELCPR	West End of London & Crystal Palace Railway
LMS	London Midland & Scottish Railway		
LNWR	London & North Western Railway	WLR	West London Railway
LSWR	London & South Western Railway	WLER	West London Extension Railway
MDR	Metropolitan District Railway		
MR	Midland Railway	WR	Western Region
NLR	North London Railway	WS&SWR	Windsor Staines & South Western Railway

A short parcels train for Kensington and Willesden waits in platform 2 at Clapham Junction on 25 June 1951 hauled by Stanier '3MT' 2-6-2T No 40204, still carrying its LMS title.
Brian Morrison

1 Clapham Junction —
The Station

'Welcome to Britain's Busiest Railway Station' proclaim the Network SouthEast signs on Clapham Junction's platforms. The name Clapham Junction has become a synonym for railway activity and complexity, but in truth the station is not in Clapham. 'Bradshaw' used always to warn travellers that it is in mid-Battersea, 1¼ miles from Clapham, a locality served by three stations on the Northern Line of the London Underground and less frequently by BR's Clapham High Street station. Moreover, today it cannot claim to be a real junction; of its daily 2,000 trains only a handful diverge at Clapham Junction. Instead, it is the passengers who have to change direction and transfer from one route to another through the station's subway or over the footbridge.

The story begins on 25 July 1834, when the London & Southampton Railway obtained an Act for a line to commence 'at the River Thames at or near Nine Elms in the parish of Battersea in the county of Surrey'. Among the Act's clauses was one protecting the water supply to Wandsworth — the company was to 'well and effectually puddle' the works through the cutting at St John's Hill. The windpump on the up side of the line remains as evidence of the wet condition of this cutting. Construction work on the line commenced in the autumn of 1834, but progress was slow until Joseph Locke succeeded Francis Giles as engineer in January 1837 and replaced the small contractors engaged on the Wandsworth section by Thomas Brassey, then at the start of his career in railway building. Hopes of opening the line from Nine Elms to Woking Common on 1 May 1838 were not realised, and public traffic eventually commenced on 21 May 1838.

To quote from a description of the start of the journey in Freeling's 1839 Guide to the London & Southampton Railway, 'We enter upon the Battersea fields, celebrated as being the first place in which

Left:
Before the days of corporate identity schemes and Network SouthEast red, white and blue signs, a variety of nameboards greeted the passenger arriving at Clapham Junction in October 1955. *British Rail*

Above:
**This view of Clapham Junction was taken from the St John's
Hill bridge in about 1870. On the left is the LSWR main line,
station building and signalbox, in the centre are the three
LBSCR tracks, and leading off to the right are the West
London Extension platforms; some fragments of mixed gauge
track can be seen here but track alterations may already
have removed part of the original layout. In the background
can be seen the LBSCR North signalbox and the viaduct
carrying the WLER to join the LSWR Windsor Line.**
Courtesy of Wandsworth Public Libraries

asparagus was raised in England, and it still supplies
vast quantities of vegetables for the London market.
The railroad passes for a considerable distance
through these market gardens . . . The rising ground
on the left is in the parish of Clapham and to the
right, about ¼-mile distant Chelsea Hospital is dis-
tinctly seen . . . Clapham Church, situated on the
common, is now broadside upon our left. The houses
on the same side upon the acclivity are in the
Wandsworth Road; many of them are handsome vil-
las, the residences of opulent London traders. We
still continue amid the market gardens, the ground
below us is under low water mark, and is consequently not infrequently invaded by floods . . . We
now cross the road from Battersea to Clapham and at
about the 2¼ mile post, enter the Wandsworth Cutting; it is nearly 1¾ miles long, in some places 45 feet
deep, and yielded 616,000 cubic yards of earth
towards the formation of the embankments; the
ascent from the 1½ mile post to just beyond the third

mile is 1 in 330. A quarter of a mile further on the
road from London to Portsmouth (St John's Hill)
passes over us by means of a handsome skew iron
bridge. This deep cutting is composed of London
clay, with beds of gravel, in which were very strong
springs of water. Passing under a bridge which bears
the road from Clapham to Wandsworth, we arrive at
Wandsworth station.'

Freeling was wrong in his description of
Wandsworth: the station was located before the
bridge, and the ticket office was situated on the down
side of the line facing the main road; steps led from
the bridge to the two platforms in the cutting below.
He continued:

'Wandsworth is one mile to the north of and Clapham
one mile and a half to the south of the station; we
now pass under two bridges of three arches each
(Trinity Road and Heathfield Road), and about a mile
further enter on the Wandle embankment.'

The next significant railway development was the
incorporation of the Richmond Railway by an Act of
21 July 1845. It was to build a line to join the main
life of the London & South Western Railway (as the
London & Southampton had now become) at the
point where the Battersea to Clapham road passed
under the railway. This road was known as Falcon
Lane, after a nearby public house (its successor still
stands at the crossroads of Falcon Road and St John's
Hill), and the junction was therefore called Falcon
Bridge Junction. The Richmond Railway was opened
on 27 July 1846 and the company was absorbed by

the LSWR on 31 December 1846. A station on this line was built in York Road, Wandsworth, nearer this small industrial town than the original station on the LSWR main line. In August 1846 the latter was consequently renamed as Clapham Common; the open

Above:
Above:
Sometime during the 1880s, this group picture was taken of the LBSCR's stationmaster at Clapham Junction and some of his staff — others would doubtless be on the night shift.
Courtesy of the National Railway Museum (612/63)

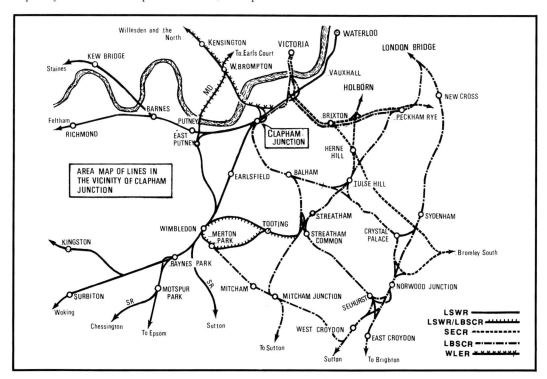

AREA MAP OF LINES IN THE VICINITY OF CLAPHAM JUNCTION

LSWR	————
LSWR/LBSCR	┼┼┼┼┼
SECR	————————
LBSCR	—·—·—·—
WLER	××××××

spaces near the station formed part of Wandsworth Common rather than Clapham Common, but the main road (now Battersea Rise) was then referred to as the Wandsworth Road or the Clapham Road and the company probably did not wish to have two stations including the name of Wandsworth.

Extension caused the Richmond Railway to become known as the Windsor Line and from August 1848 it was provided with an up track independent of the main line from Falcon Bridge Junction towards Nine Elms; separation of the down lines did not take place until August 1860. However, Falcon Bridge Junction remained as an exchange point, and the LSWR acquired some four acres of land between the main and Windsor lines. The August 1857 working

timetable shows trains of empty 'foreign' wagons from Godalming and Portsmouth terminating at 'Clapham or Falcon Junction', where they would be collected by Nine Elms to Willesden Junction freight trains routed via Old Kew Junction and the North & South Western Junction Railway, opened in 1853.

Meanwhile, another railway company had plans to run through Wandsworth. The London & Brighton Railway had become dissatisfied with the tolls imposed on its traffic by the London & Croydon company. Therefore, in 1845, it proposed to build its own line from Croydon to join the LSWR at Wandsworth and to share that company's planned Metropolitan Extension to Waterloo, one reason why the LSWR provided four tracks into its new terminus. The L&B obtained powers for this line on 27 July 1846 and agreed to pay the LSWR in perpetuity 70% of its gross earnings from traffic over the Waterloo extension. This formed part of a wider agreement between the companies limiting territorial expansion in Surrey and Sussex. However, the amalgamation later in 1846 of the Brighton and Croydon companies to form the London Brighton & South Coast Railway removed the incentive to construct the link with the LSWR.

So it was a small independent company, the West End of London & Crystal Palace Railway which now brought another line into the Wandsworth area. The removal of the Crystal Palace from Hyde Park to Sydenham had raised expectations of excursion and residential traffic, and this railway company proposed to build a line from Crystal Palace to join the LSWR at Falcon Junction, Wandsworth, with branches from Crystal Palace to Norwood Junction and from Battersea to a Thameside wharf near the new Chelsea suspension bridge. It was intended that the LSWR should work the line, but final agreement between LSWR and WELCP broke down over South Western opposition to the Thameside branch.

The WELCP obtained its Act on 4 August 1853 and made an agreement with the LBSCR to work its line; subsequently the LBSCR leased the line in 1858 and purchased the company outright from 1 July 1859. Despite this link with the LBSCR, the WELCP still wanted to run into Waterloo and an agreement was reached with the LSWR in 1855 for Crystal Palace trains to have their separate terminus near York Road, to be built by the LSWR. However, the LSWR had difficulty in finding the land for this station and the LBSCR, as the operator of the WELCP, decided that Waterloo could not handle this extra traffic.

The WELCP reverted to its original intentions and on 1 December 1856 opened the first section of its line from Crystal Palace to a temporary terminus at Wandsworth Common, beyond Nightingale Lane and to the west of the present station. The trains were worked by the LBSCR as an extension of its London Bridge to Crystal Palace service.

On 29 March 1858 the WELCP completed its line by opening from Wandsworth Common to Pimlico, the name given to its passenger terminus on the south bank of the Thames at Battersea Wharf. The original station at Wandsworth Common closed on 1 June 1858, having already been replaced by one on the

Below:
A view taken in the opposite direction, also about 1900, shows a LBSCR 'B2' 4-4-0 approaching with a train on the up local line. To the left can be seen Falcon Junction where the WLER tracks joined the LBSCR; beyond St John's Hill bridge is the Brighton's elevated South box, while the upper splitting arms of the LSWR's down starting signal controlled the entrance to the quadruple track beyond.
Ian Allan Library

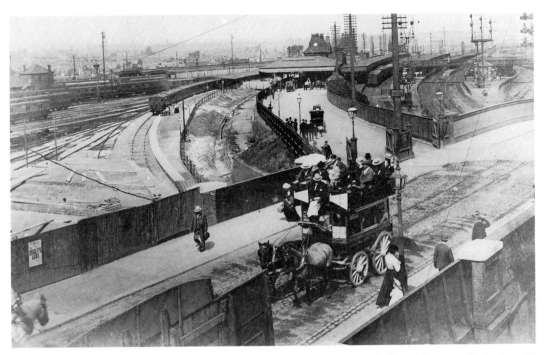

Above:
This picture was probably taken from the LBSCR South box during 1902 while the LSWR main line tracks were being widened. The new up loop platform (later No 4) is already in use and linked by temporary awnings and gangways to the station building. Meanwhile, the site of the new up local and through lines is being excavated. To the left of the Clapham omnibus, behind the hoardings, the new LSWR entrance from St John's Hill is being built, soon to replace the slope shown here. The old Windsor Line platforms can be seen in the left background. A local train is standing in the new loop platform as the up main is occupied by a varied collection of vehicles, probably a milk train.
Courtesy of the National Railway Museum (497/55)

extension called New Wandsworth, 60 chains nearer Pimlico. This station was situated to the south of Freemasons bridge on the opposite side of the road to the LSWR's Clapham Common station. Originally built with two platforms, these were reached by steps from the bridge and from the down side station building located in a short cul-de-sac leading off Battersea Rise. Subsequently this provided access to the LBSCR's high level New Wandsworth goods yard. (Freemasons bridge gained its name from the nearby Royal Masonic School and the [then] Freemasons Arms public house.) From New Wandsworth, the WELCP line ran parallel to the LSWR for over a mile without making any connection, then turned to dive under it at Stewarts Lane before reaching its riverside terminus.

Extension from the WELCP at Stewarts Lane across the Thames into the West End was achieved by the

Victoria Station & Pimlico Railway, authorised on 23 July 1858. Its opening on 1 October 1860 to Victoria station, on the site of the Grosvenor Canal basin, replaced Pimlico as the passenger terminus. Ownership of Victoria was divided between the LBSCR (50%), Great Western Railway (25%) and the London Chatham & Dover Railway (25%). The gradual advance of the LCDR from East Kent towards London was then completed on 3 December 1860, when its trains began to run into Victoria over the WELCP line. The LCDR was not allowed to take local traffic and so its trains ran non-stop between Victoria and Crystal Palace. However, LCDR use of the WELCP was short-lived, ceasing when its main line via Herne Hill was opened throughout on 1 July 1863.

To shorten its circuitous route into Victoria from Norwood Junction via Crystal Palace, the LBSCR obtained powers on 3 July 1860 for a direct line from Windmill Bridge Junction outside Croydon to join the WELCP at Balham; this was opened on 1 December 1862.

After these developments, the creation of Clapham Junction itself was due to the arrival of another small company, the West London Extension Railway. In 1844 the West London Railway had been built to link Kensington and its canal with the London & North Western Railway at Willesden Junction and the Great Western at Old Oak Common. It became known as 'Mr Punch's Railway' from its unreliability, until leased jointly by the LNWR and GWR in 1846 and acquired by them in 1854. Clearly the key to its ultimate success lay in a connection to the railways south of the Thames. The two northern companies

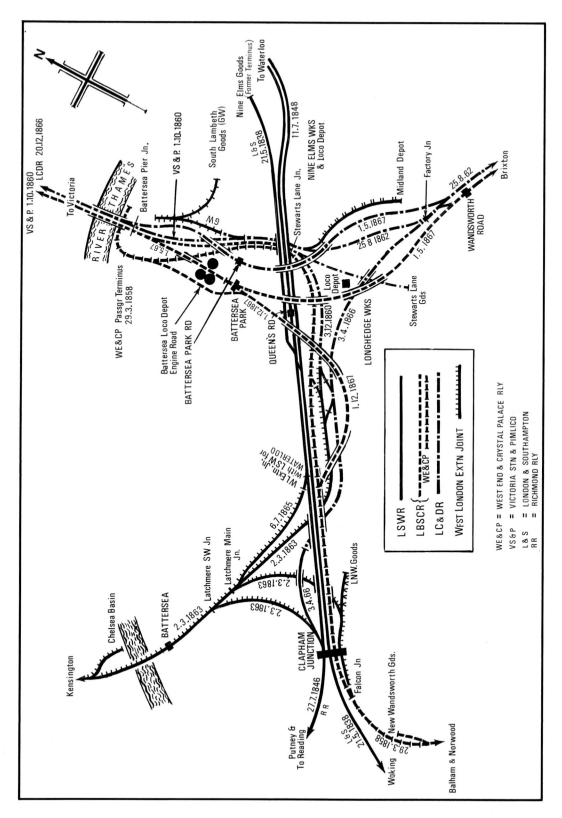

Above:
The frontage of the LSWR entrance in St John's Hill, with the district offices at No 56 just visible on the left. Horse traction for the LCC trams (right) between Clapham Junction and Wandsworth lasted until December 1909.
Commercial postcard — A.A.Jackson collection

therefore invited the LSWR and the LBSCR to take part in a new joint company with a capital of £300,000; the LNWR and the GWR would each hold one third and the two southern companies one sixth each. The WLER obtained its Act on 13 August 1859.

The main line of the WLER made an end-on junction with the West London to the east of that company's Kensington station (subsequently known as Addison Road and later as Olympia). The line crossed the Thames by the Cremorne bridge at Chelsea to reach Latchmere Junction in Battersea. Here the mixed gauge main line continued to Longhedge Junction, where it joined the WELCP line to Victoria. However, it is two of the branches from Latchmere Junction which first concern us. Branch No 1 of 59 chains passed under the parallel LSWR and LBSCR main lines to join the latter at Falcon Junction — a rather confusing title as the junction was adjacent to the St John's Hill overbridge rather than to the Falcon Lane underbridge. This branch was mixed gauge, though there is no evidence that GWR broad gauge trains ever used it. Branch No 2 of 38 chains curved sharply round from Latchmere Junction to join the Windsor Line of the LSWR shortly before Falcon Lane bridge. The main line of the WLER and these two curves came into use on 2 March 1863.

The LCDR was not a partner in the WLER and did not succeed in obtaining running powers over it. It

needed connections with the other companies, and so on 14 July 1864 it was authorised to build a line from Factory Junction on its Victoria-Herne Hill route to Longhedge Junction, thence alongside the WLER main line and under the LBSCR and LSWR tracks, where it diverged to join the WLER's No 2 branch and the LSWR Windsor Line at a point then termed Ludgate Junction. This line was opened for freight traffic on 1 March 1866 and for passenger trains on 3 April. The 40 chains of this line between Ludgate Junction and the bridge under the LSWR main line were transferred to that company's ownership by an Act of 5 July 1865. The LSWR had contributed £316,000 to the cost of the LCDR's Metropolitan Extension in exchange for running powers to its City station at Ludgate Hill.

To enable passengers off the LSWR and LBSCR to interchange with the WLER and LCDR a new junction station was needed — in fact each line came to have its own individual station, linked only by a common subway. Firstly, on the LSWR Windsor Line side, two terminal platforms and sidings for the Kensington trains were separated by more sidings and a carriage shed from the two platforms serving trains to and from Waterloo. The LSWR main line swept round the curve from under St John's Hill to leave a space between it and the Windsor Line which was also occupied by carriage sidings. A slope from St John's Hill led to the LSWR booking office and principal station buildings on the up main line platform. The LSWR's down main line platform was an island with the LBSCR up main track at the other face.

At this time, the LBSCR had already begun to widen the WELCP line and had added a second up road for local traffic which had a narrow single-sided platform between the two up lines at the Victoria end of the station. The Brighton's down platform was another island with the WLER departure line at its outer face, and finally there was that company's arrival platform. Both these tracks were WLER prop-

Below left:
To take this picture the photographer may have climbed during the summer of 1907 on to the girders being erected to carry the new LSWR Clapham Junction East (later 'A') box. The temporary 1906-built East box stands at the end of the rebuilt Windsor Line platforms, and the track of the future down through line awaits completion of the new layout in October to be brought into service. An up main line local train headed by a 'M7' 0-4-4T is leaving the station. On the Brighton side a Stroudley 0-4-2 is running tender first down the fast line with a train of six-wheelers — perhaps an empty working to Eardley sidings. *Ian Allan Library*

Below:
The photographer has turned round on his perch to take the view towards London. On the extreme left an Adams 4-4-2T is approaching Ludgate Junction with a train from Kensington. The tracks for the realigned Windsor lines have been laid between the existing local roads, while a suburban train heads towards Waterloo on the up Windsor through. Alongside it, a restaurant car train (perhaps empty stock) takes the one and only up main line into the terminus, passing a down West of England express hauled by a 'L12' 4-4-0. On the right, a LBSCR van and a LSWR coach await collection from the transfer siding.
Commercial postcard — Author's collection

Clapham Junction 1866

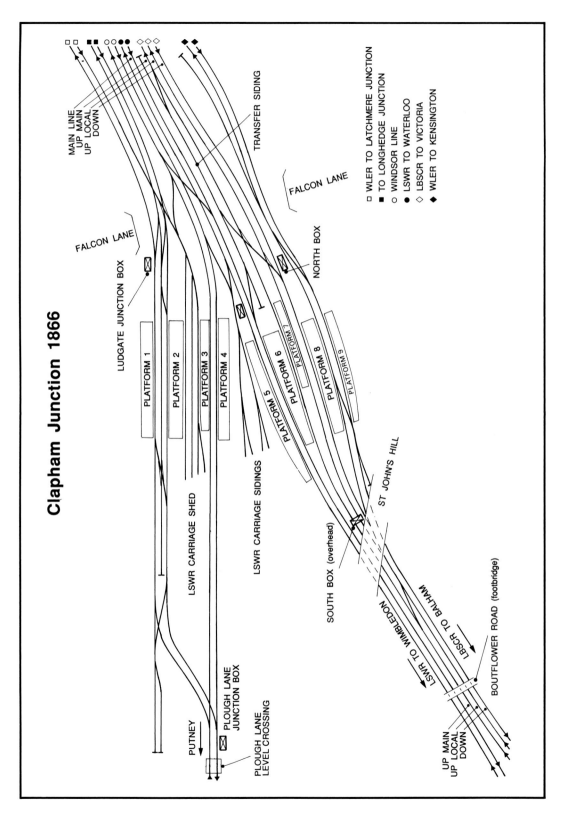

MAIN LINE
UP MAIN
UP LOCAL
DOWN

TRANSFER SIDING

FALCON LANE

☐ WLER TO LATCHMERE JUNCTION
■ TO LONGHEDGE JUNCTION
○ WINDSOR LINE
● LSWR TO WATERLOO
◇ LBSCR TO VICTORIA
◆ WLER TO KENSINGTON

FALCON LANE

NORTH BOX

LUDGATE JUNCTION BOX

PLATFORM 1

PLATFORM 2

PLATFORM 3

PLATFORM 4

LSWR CARRIAGE SHED

LSWR CARRIAGE SIDINGS

PLATFORM 5

PLATFORM 6

PLATFORM 7

PLATFORM 8

PLATFORM 9

SOUTH BOX (overhead)

ST JOHN'S HILL

LSWR TO WIMBLEDON

LBSCR TO BALHAM

BOUTFLOWER ROAD (footbridge)

UP MAIN
UP LOCAL
DOWN

PUTNEY

PLOUGH LANE JUNCTION BOX

PLOUGH LANE LEVEL CROSSING

Above:
A view of LSWR main line platforms 4 and 5, also showing the milk dock and footbridge to St John's Hill entrance, taken on 3 December 1909. *British Rail*

erty, unlike the Kensington platforms on the other side of the station which belonged to the LSWR. All platforms were connected by a passenger subway which led to the LBSCR booking office in Prested Road, a side street near the bottom of St John's Hill.

It was decided to call the new station Clapham Junction, probably in succession to the LSWR's Clapham Common station, which closed simultaneously with the opening of Clapham Junction on 2 March 1863. However, the LBSCR did not close its New Wandsworth passenger station until 1 November 1869. A transfer siding was built between the down South Western and up Brighton lines at the London end of the station for the exchange of horse boxes and miscellaneous coaching traffic from one company to the other.

When the LCDR/LSWR line from Longhedge Junction to Ludgate Junction was opened in 1866, the Ludgate Hill trains used the Kensington platforms at Clapham Junction and in order to cater for through trains from the Thames Valley to the City, the Kensington tracks were then extended to join the principal Windsor lines at Plough Lane level crossing, about 400 yards west of the station.

When the Kingston to Ludgate Hill service via Richmond was succeeded in 1869 by one via Wimbledon, the junction at Plough Lane was no longer required. With increasing rail and road traffic, it was decided to replace the level crossing by an underbridge to the north of the existing line and to raise the Windsor Line tracks and divert them to the north side of the carriage sidings, with new platforms adjacent to the Kensington station. This work was completed on 20 March 1876 and the old course of the Windsor

Line was then absorbed into the growing area of Clapham yard. However, the Kensington sidings beyond the West London platform (now No 2) still remain at the original lower level.

Clapham Junction station soon attracted complaints from passengers. At the LSWR General Meeting in February 1874, a shareholder said 'I think that a more disgraceful station is not to be found connected with any railway in this country, considering the amount of traffic passing through it. I do not know how many persons are laid up with colds caught at that station.' (An opinion probably shared by present-day users of platform 11.) The station building on the up main line platform was subsequently enlarged and embellished in the French Renaissance manner, though much of the roof ornamentation was removed during further reconstruction after 1900. In conjunction with its widening between Clapham Junction and Wimbledon, the LSWR continued its additional up local line into the station on 5 October 1885, making the up platform (No 5) into an island. In 1893 the company tried to relieve the gloom in the long subway by adding tiling and skylights.

Both companies were finding that Clapham Junction station was a bottleneck. The LBSCR therefore obtained powers on 4 August 1890 to quadruple its

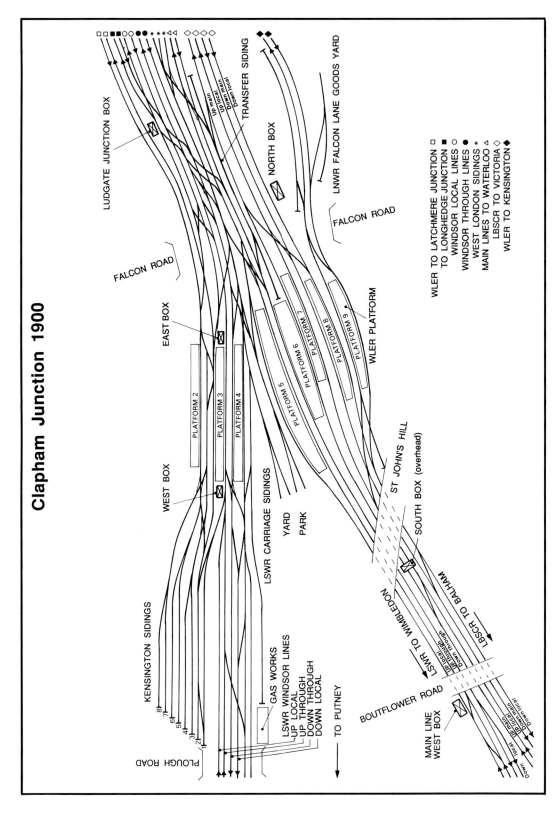

Clapham Junction 1900

LUDGATE JUNCTION BOX

Up main
Up local
Down main
Down local

TRANSFER SIDING

NORTH BOX

LNWR FALCON LANE GOODS YARD

FALCON ROAD

FALCON ROAD

EAST BOX

WEST BOX

PLATFORM 2

PLATFORM 3

PLATFORM 4

PLATFORM 5

PLATFORM 6

PLATFORM 7

PLATFORM 8

PLATFORM 9

WLER PLATFORM

LSWR CARRIAGE SIDINGS

YARD

PARK

ST JOHN'S HILL

SOUTH BOX (overhead)

LSWR TO WIMBLEDON

LBSCR TO BALHAM

Up local
Up through
Down through
Down local

KENSINGTON SIDINGS

GAS WORKS

LSWR WINDSOR LINES
UP LOCAL
UP THROUGH
DOWN THROUGH
DOWN LOCAL

8
7
6
5
4
3
2
1

TO PUTNEY

BOUTFLOWER ROAD

MAIN LINE
WEST BOX

PLOUGH ROAD

Up main
Up local
Down main
Down local

Down

□□ ■■○○ ●● ***◁◁ ◇◇◇◇ ◆◆

□ WLER TO LATCHMERE JUNCTION
□ TO LONGHEDGE JUNCTION
■ WINDSOR LOCAL LINES
○ WINDSOR THROUGH LINES
● WEST LONDON SIDINGS
* MAIN LINES TO WATERLOO
◁ LBSCR TO VICTORIA
◇ WLER TO KENSINGTON
◆

20

line through the station and this was done by taking the new down local line along the outer face of the existing down platform, hitherto used for Kensington departures, and converting the WLER arrival platform into an island for West London traffic in both directions. The problem then was to squeeze the extra down line through the deep cutting beyond the St John's Hill bridge, where the grounds of the Royal Masonic School for Girls overlooked the railway. To avoid taking land from the school, the retaining wall behind the widening was surmounted by an overhanging parapet supported by buttresses (which eventually became unsafe and had to be removed in 1981 with consequent delay and diversion of traffic). The widening came into use during the summer of 1895, and at the same time a footpath was provided from St John's Hill to join the flimsy footbridge linking the WLER, LBSCR and down LSWR platforms at this end of the station.

The LBSCR now had four roads through the station, but the LSWR had only one track for down main line traffic, while on the Windsor Line the four tracks on each side of Clapham Junction converged into the station's up and down platforms. The company admitted that fast trains were continually being delayed by stopping services, so obtained powers for widening and reconstruction in its Act of 6 August 1897, the cost being estimated at about £121,000. First of all, land had to be acquired from Battersea Grammar School to extend the carriage sidings towards Plough Road, as well as to provide new sidings at Wimbledon Park intended to relieve Clapham Yard of suburban traffic.

Work started in late 1900 to lengthen St John's Hill bridge for two additional tracks, and the first stage of rebuilding was to construct a new 700ft island platform (new No 4). The up local line was diverted to the outer face of this to allow the existing No 5 plat-

form to be enlarged in length to 900ft and in width to 60ft, while the space between platforms 4 and 5 was to be laid out to accommodate the future up local and up through lines. This work involved the severance of the road approach from St John's Hill, which was replaced by a pedestrian footbridge leading to a ticket office above the platforms. The resited up lines came into use early in 1903, enabling the original up and down tracks to become from 26 April a pair of down lines. The temporary up local line along the outer face of platform 4 then became a loop line, used mainly for milk and parcels traffic, but during World War 1 it frequently received ambulance trains from Southampton Docks. Beyond No 4 were milk docks connected by lift to the parcels office and covered courtyard in St John's Hill. No 5 platform retained some of its original buildings at platform level, including the refreshment room and the station superintendent's office.

Meanwhile, work had started to relieve the Windsor Line bottleneck. The 1897 Act had authorised the LSWR to divert the WLER, to widen Falcon Road bridge and acquire land for a northward extension of the station. Work began there in May 1901 — firstly to build a new viaduct to carry a 700ft by 30ft island platform (No 1) for Kensington traffic, which came into use on 24 June 1906. The original Kensington departure platform was then reconstructed as another 700ft island (No 2) for up Windsor Line trains, completed on 4 November 1906. Finally island platform No 3 for the down Windsor Line took the site of the old No 3, which had accommodated Kensington

Below:
The ex-LBSCR 1910 station building and forecourt at St John's Hill, photographed on 20 July 1967. *Author*

Above:
This 27 August 1978 picture shows the ex-LSWR 'C' (originally Windsor Line West) signalbox built for pneumatic operation in 1911. A Weybridge to Waterloo via Hounslow train is approaching.
Ian Allan Library — Brian Morrison

Right:
The lower level of the Kensington sidings, compared with the Windsor lines rising to cross Plough Road, is evident in this picture of No 73127 marshalling the Morden and Vauxhall to St Erth milk tank train on 18 August 1976.
Ian Allan Library — R.E.Ruffell

Below right:
On 11 May 1958, 'U' class 2-6-0 No 31624 propels the Nine Elms crane through the transfer siding following engineering work on the Central section. *Author*

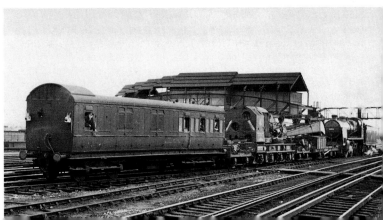

arrivals and up Windsor Line traffic. Its outer face came into use on 24 March 1907 and the inner side on 13 October 1907, simultaneously with the rearrangement of the Windsor Line tracks. The original down Windsor platform (old No 4) was then demolished and its site added to the carriage sidings.

The LSWR also owned property in St John's Hill — some of these houses were occupied by senior officers and two by the Main Line and Metropolitan district offices. Under the Herbert Walker regime these offices were amalgamated and transferred to Waterloo; 56 St John's Hill then became the residence of the Clapham Junction station superintendent, a post of silk hat status, responsible in 1919 for 180 staff. His LBSCR colleague with 76 employees only wore the usual peaked cap at this period.

In June 1907 the station subway was extended to a new north side entrance in Winstanley Road, where an additional LSWR booking office and a cab yard were provided. The new footbridge which had been erected over the main line platforms in 1903-05 was continued to the Windsor side in 1907; it was of ample width and lifts served each platform.

In addition to this series of works, the reconstruction was influenced by an accident at the station. Back in September 1900 two LBSCR porters had been run down by a train while transferring luggage between the Brighton's up and down platforms. One was killed and the other terribly mutilated. The next day the platform staff of both companies addressed a petition to the President of the Board of Trade. They said that the station subway and the narrow LBSCR footbridge were too congested to use for baggage transfer; in addition to passengers' luggage and parcel traffic, over 100 loaded milk churns had to be manhandled daily across as many as five tracks, with little warning of up trains coming out of the cutting. They concluded, 'Our lives are nothing but a series of thrilling adventures and hairbreadth escapes'.

In response to this plea, the Board of Trade ensured that the LSWR's plans for the station reconstruction would eliminate all transfers at track level, but the LBSCR merely offered some vague assurances. Although it already had four tracks through Clapham Junction, the company's main up platform (shared with the LSWR) was narrow, and even more cramped was the staggered up local line platform situated between the two up lines. The rearrangement of tracks between Battersea Park and Balham carried out in 1907/08 left the original layout in situ at Clapham Junction, so that the up local line had to cross the down main at each end of the station.

The LBSCR therefore commenced a major reconstruction of the station. Once again the WLER tracks were shifted further to the south; the new arrival platform (No 12) came into use on 27 June 1909 and the departure platform (No 11) on 7 November. The other face of this island (No 10) then became the Brighton's down local platform. The central island was reconstructed and enlarged to accommodate the up local at No 9 on 13 March 1910 (when the rearrangement of the tracks was carried out), and the widened No 8 on the other side continued to serve the down main. No 7 still handled up main line trains, and as the two companies had not co-ordinated their rebuilding, it remained as a narrow platform with flimsy wooden buildings and awnings.

Otherwise the new LBSCR platform buildings were more substantial than those on the LSWR side, with refreshment rooms provided on both down platforms. A wide footbridge with luggage lifts linked all the Brighton platforms to the LSWR footbridge and to a new high level booking office in St John's Hill, which formed part of a quite prominent and attractive station building. Unfortunately the footbridge had a deep corrugated iron roof which did not match the adjacent South Western structure. LSWR passengers could enter the station here but were kept to one side of a divided gangway which led to their own booking office. Below the LBSCR booking office was its parcels office with a low level yard and access to a milk dock served by No 12 platform. Another Brighton ticket office in the station subway replaced the original office in Prested Road, while the LSWR had its own main line booking office further along the subway. Apart from war and fire damage, most of the platform buildings dating from the 1900-10 reconstruction remain in existence today.

Electrification brought few changes to the station itself: the LBSCR's local lines were electrified on the 6,700-volt 25-cycle ac overhead system from 12 May 1911. One of the Pig Hill sidings alongside the WLER was wired as an emergency turnback facility, and subsequently the through lines were equipped, again mainly for possible diversions rather than for regular traffic. The last ac trains ran on 22 September 1929, but it is still possible to see the foundations and base of some of the overhead gantries in the cutting towards Wandsworth Common.

The LSWR adopted the 600 volt dc third rail system and a 5,625kW rotary converter sub-station was built at the down end of platform 5 under the gangway to St John's Hill. This was superseded by rectifier sub-stations elsewhere during the 1950s. The first LSWR electric trains ran on the Windsor Line on 25 October 1915 and on the main line on 30 January 1916. As part of the Southern Railway's policy of standardisation, the third rail came into use on the ex-LBSCR lines at Clapham Junction from 3 March 1929.

Electrification was extended to the West London platforms (now Nos 16 and 17) on 9 September 1968 — initially to terminate peak hour trains during the reconstruction of underline bridges at Longhedge and Queenstown Road, but subsequently for both peak hour and weekend services during the Victoria resignalling and the construction of the raft above the platforms to facilitate property development. On the

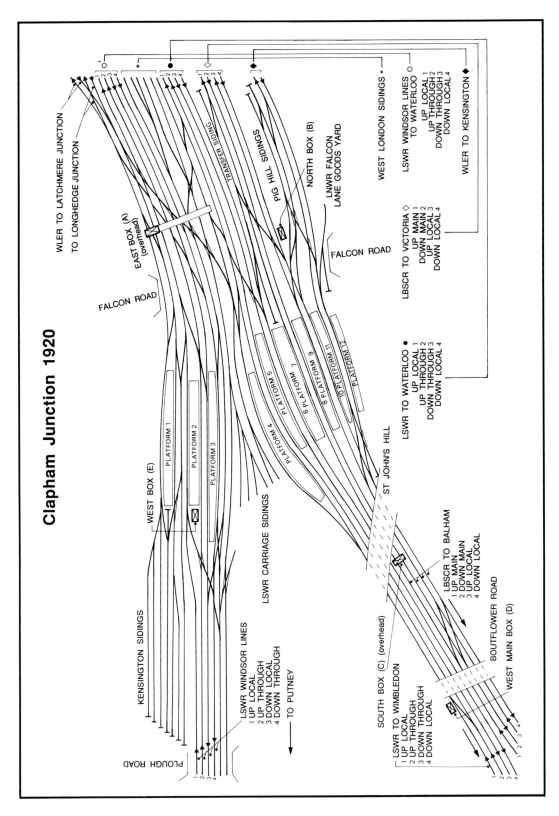

Clapham Junction 1920

WLER TO LATCHMERE JUNCTION

TO LONGHEDGE JUNCTION

EAST BOX (A) (overhead)

TRANSFER SIDING

PIG HILL SIDINGS

NORTH BOX (B)

LNWR FALCON
LANE GOODS YARD

FALCON ROAD

FALCON ROAD

WEST LONDON SIDINGS *

LSWR WINDSOR LINES
TO WATERLOO ○
 UP LOCAL 1
 UP THROUGH 2
 DOWN THROUGH 3
 DOWN LOCAL 4

WLER TO KENSINGTON ◆

LBSCR TO VICTORIA ◇
 UP MAIN 1
 DOWN MAIN 2
 UP LOCAL 3
 DOWN LOCAL 4

LSWR TO WATERLOO ●
 UP LOCAL 1
 UP THROUGH 2
 DOWN THROUGH 3
 DOWN LOCAL 4

ST JOHN'S HILL

LBSCR TO BALHAM
 1 UP MAIN
 2 DOWN MAIN
 3 UP LOCAL
 4 DOWN LOCAL

BOUTFLOWER ROAD

WEST MAIN BOX (D)

LSWR TO WIMBLEDON
 1 UP LOCAL
 2 UP THROUGH
 3 DOWN THROUGH
 4 DOWN LOCAL

SOUTH BOX (C) (overhead)

WEST BOX (E)

PLATFORM 1

PLATFORM 2

PLATFORM 3

LSWR CARRIAGE SIDINGS

PLATFORM 4

PLATFORM 5

6 PLATFORM 7

8 PLATFORM 9

10 PLATFORM 11

PLATFORM 12

KENSINGTON SIDINGS

LSWR WINDSOR LINES
 1 UP LOCAL
 2 UP THROUGH
 3 DOWN LOCAL
 4 DOWN THROUGH

TO PUTNEY

PLOUGH ROAD

24

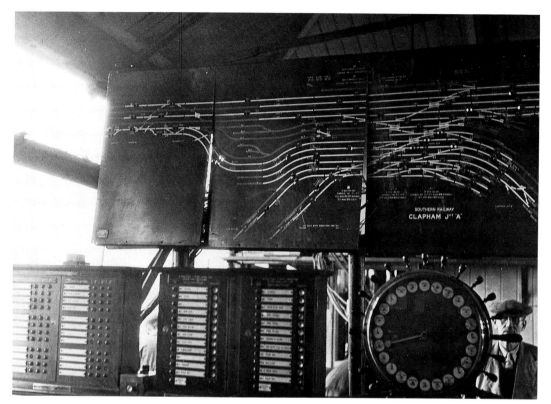

Clapham Junction 'A' box. This interior shows the track
diagram, magazine type train describers for South Western
lines, and a rotary describer to Longhedge Junction. The
picture was taken after enemy action on 15 October 1940.
British Rail

South Western side, the up main loop had not been
electrified as it was used only by milk and parcels
trains, but with the end of steam in 1967 this road
(now platform 7) was equipped, together with many
of the carriage sidings. It was still unusual to see an
electric train in platform 7, until, in 1986, fast main
line trains began to call at Clapham Junction and it
was realised that the superelevation of the curve on
the up through line (platform 8) made it difficult for
passengers to alight on that side.

Originally both companies numbered their platforms in one common series, but after the rebuilding
of 1909-10 the Brighton allotted its numbers to platform faces, while the South Western numbers still
denoted complete platforms, thus LSWR 1 to 6 and
LBSCR 7 to 12. It took the Southern Railway almost
the whole of its existence to end this anomaly; on 16
November 1947 the platform faces were renumbered
1 to 17. One result of Grouping was the closure of the
LSWR entrance in St John's Hill, passengers being
diverted to the LBSCR building lower down the hill.
The overhead walkway to the LSWR booking office
was converted into a staff training school, and the
parcels courtyard became a transfer point for milk
pumped out from tank wagons standing in the docks
below. The LSWR forecourt is now used as a turning
point for buses terminating at Clapham Junction, and
the former station superintendent's residence currently houses the Area Signal Engineer.

In May 1936, as part of the South Western section
resignalling, tracks were rearranged between Wimbledon and Waterloo. The up local line at platform 4
(inner face) became the up through, the adjacent up
through became the down through, and on the other
side of platform 5 the up local took over the former
down through track; only the down local alongside
platform 6 remained unaffected. A summary of the
changes in Clapham Junction's platforms follows this
chapter.

Clapham Junction station suffered badly during the
1940-41 'blitz'. During the first night of heavy bombing, on 8 September 1940, there was a direct hit on
the carriage shed below the Granada cinema and several coaches were badly damaged. The station was
again a target for the night raid of 13/14 September;
one bomb damaged the roof and interior of 'A' box,
another bomb nearby fell between the up Windsor
Line and the Kensington platforms, blocking both
lines, while a delayed action bomb was suspected on
the western section down main through platform (No

5). This exploded early on the 14th, blocking the through lines, but enabling traffic to resume elsewhere. At this time Waterloo was closed to all traffic except mail and newspaper trains and Clapham Junction was acting as the Western Section terminus.

Trains had hardly started running again, when workmen clearing the debris on platform 5 found signs of another unexploded bomb there. An Army officer arrived to confirm this and said he would call a bomb disposal squad — the hours passed and one did not appear. Following anxious enquiries by the SR, after midnight, it was found that the bomb had not been reported. When the disposal unit eventually arrived at daybreak on the 15th, its investigation revealed the presence of a 500lb bomb — and that until it could be removed, the whole station had to be closed. Before anything could be done, the bomb exploded, demolishing part of the buildings and awnings on platform 5 and scattering debris across all the South Western main line tracks, clearance of which took several days. As for permanent repairs, passengers still emerge from the subway on to what is now platforms 9 and 10 to find themselves exposed to the elements!

Other bombs had wreaked havoc elsewhere in the vicinity of Clapham Junction — one had struck the bridge carrying the Windsor Line tracks over the lines from Kensington and Clapham Junction to Longhedge Junction, blocking all three important routes. At Pouparts Junction nearby, a dangerous delayed action bomb halted all traffic towards Waterloo and Victoria until the Army dealt with it in a controlled explosion on 19 September. Later that autumn, on 13 October, the Plough Road bridge under the Windsor Lines was hit; single line working was restored the following day, but it was a fortnight before all four tracks were available again.

These are only a few of the many incidents due to enemy action affecting Clapham Junction during World War 2; often the station became the London terminus when Waterloo or Victoria was out of action — also, however, trains from Waterloo could sometimes get no further than Clapham as the cutting seemed to be a favourite resting place for unexploded bombs.

The venerable wooden buildings and awnings on platforms 11 and 12, which had escaped both companies' reconstruction, were at last demolished during 1967 and replaced by glass screens and an exiguous steel-framed canopy. Demolition during the 1960s also removed the LSWR electrical sub-station building, that company's former parcels office in St John's Hill and the overhead passage to the station.

Despite other platform rationalisations, the station subway was still a public thoroughfare, requiring ticket barriers at every platform stairway. As an economy measure, authority was obtained to convert it into a closed passage for rail travellers only as from 7 September 1969. Therefore the ex-LBSCR and ex-LSWR booking offices in the subway and that in the former Brighton station building in St John's Hill were all shut, to be replaced by a modest single-storey ticket office in Prested Road, adjacent to the new barriers at the end of the subway. The ex-LSWR Windsor Line booking office was retained to serve the Winstanley Road entrance.

In 1979 a buffet was opened for down Windsor Line passengers on platforms 5 and 6 (the South Western main line buffet had disappeared in the bombing). Then, from 13 April 1980, platform 1 was taken out of use and all Kensington trains now started from platform 2. More eventfully, on the evening of 8 July 1981 a fire broke out above platforms 9 and 10; as a result the last traces of the gangway from St John's Hill were removed as well as more of the awnings from these platforms. This fire damage to the footbridge was repaired as part of a general refurbishment of the platform buildings and canopies which was carried out between 1983 and 1986. The timberwork of the LSWR footbridge has been attractively set off in red paint and forms a contrast to the grim LBSCR structure beyond; this has needed strengthening with a false floor, adding another step to the platform staircases.

In 1919, the approach from St John's Hill to the station subway was through what was described as a parade of good shops — Hamilton Ellis mentioned a barber's shop there which seated its customers in ex-Pullman car swivel chairs. However, by the 1970s this area had seen better days and was an attractive site for developers anxious to build office blocks next to a major railway station. Therefore, in 1986, work started on a redevelopment scheme in collaboration with the Charterhall Group which provided BR with the finance for a £1 million modernisation of the station.

The Prested Road ticket office and most of the subway were closed from 22 March 1986, so the Brighton entrance from St John's Hill had to be reopened with a temporary ticket office (the original buildings here were in a state of progressive decay). Making the sub-

way watertight and relining it with ornamental tiling
was a protracted task and finally there were delays in
the completion of the shopping mall, 'The Junction',
which now links St John's Hill with the station
entrance. There is also a vehicular approach from
Falcon Road and a small car park. The subway and
new ticket office eventually opened on 1 August 1988
and a short-lived travel centre a month later. For the
greater inconvenience of passengers, all platform
level toilets were replaced by a facility in the subway
with a pay-as-you-enter turnstile. Modernisation was
completed in June 1990 by a £1.49 million scheme in
co-operation with the London Borough of
Wandsworth, which saw the reopening of the northern end of the subway into a new steel and glass
booking hall facing Winstanley Road, an area now of
up-market development, where a number of minibus
routes terminate. The arches under the Kensington
platform have been refurbished to house shops and
small businesses.

Physical linkage between the LSWR and the LBSCR
at Clapham Junction was limited to the transfer siding, which made trailing connections with the South
Western's down local line and the Brighton's up
through line. The interchange of individual vehicles
dwindled steadily, but during the 1950s, when SR
designed Class 12 diesel shunters began to work in
Nine Elms yard, they returned each weekend to Norwood Junction shed via the transfer siding. Subsequently, Class 42 and 47 diesels working on the
South Western Division main lines used the same
route to reach Selhurst for servicing.

Left:

In the autumn of 1947 it was the turn of the South Western tracks to be dealt with. Here, beneath the arch of Freemasons Bridge on 19 October, the layers of new ballast have been laid for the up through line and the track is being lowered into position. A 'Q1' 0-6-0 stands by on the down line with the engineers' train. *British Rail*

Following the closure of Nine Elms loco depot in July 1967 and of the goods yard a year later, both sites were acquired for the new Covent Garden market. It was thought that the proximity of the main line would encourage the market authority to provide a rail terminal for produce imported via the Dunkerque-Dover train ferry. These trains would probably run via Redhill to Clapham Junction, where a direct running connection would be required between the Central and South Western lines. During 1970 the transfer siding was removed and a three-stage ladder crossover installed between the Central through lines and the South Western local lines. This came into service in May 1971 and was used occa-

Left:

Lack of track maintenance during the war meant that waterlogged formations had to be excavated and then renewed by the process known as 'blanketing'. On 30 March 1947 the Central section through lines on the New Wandsworth side of Freemasons Bridge are receiving attention. *British Rail*

sionally by the diesel locos en route between Waterloo and Selhurst depot. However, the market authority showed no interest in a rail connection, and the available site has been occupied by various warehouses. Instead, the streets of South London see a nightly invasion of Continental juggernaut lorries. The only revenue-earning train to use the connection appears to have been a troop special on 1 August 1971 from Chesterfield to Crowborough which ran via Waterloo to change engines. Having fallen into disuse, the pointwork was gradually dismantled and no provision for a connection was made in the Victoria resignalling scheme.

According to a plan of 1859, there was a switch house controlling the divergence of the LSWR down main and Windsor lines, while the earliest photographs of the new Clapham Junction station show a LSWR box at the east end of the up main line platform. As part of the changes on the Windsor lines made in 1876, what was described as the high East box was built at the Waterloo end of the up Windsor/Kensington arrival platform (No 3); this had 55 levers in 1876 and 61 in 1885, controlling the whole

of the east end of the station. In relation to today's layout this box was situated at the Waterloo end of the present platform 6. At the other end of the up Windsor platform was the 17-lever West box. A short distance east of the station was Ludgate Junction box which worked the junction of the Kensington and Longhedge lines with the Windsor goods (later slow) lines from Nine Elms. The main line West box (22 levers), in the cutting near Freemasons bridge, controlled the start (after 1884) of the quadruple track towards Wimbledon. The main and Windsor lines were closer together at this time and were linked by crossovers at Ludgate Junction.

The high East box stood in the way of the rearrangement of tracks on the Windsor Line and was replaced on 24 June 1906 by a temporary 101 lever cabin mounted on a gantry at the east end of the Windsor Line platforms. However the LSWR had already decided to adopt pneumatic signalling throughout the Clapham Junction area; it would save space compared with mechanical interlocking, provide quicker operation and enable Ludgate Junction box to be abolished, though the anticipated savings in cost were not realised. Power for the low pressure pneumatic system was generated from a plant near Plough Road. The first pneumatic cabin was the small (10 lever) main line West box which came into service on 21 May 1911, followed by the Windsor Line West box (34 levers) a week later. The new East box was erected on a bridge spanning the Windsor tracks a little to the east of the temporary box. Its 39-lever main line frame came into use on 28 January 1912, and the 44-lever Windsor Line frame on 4 February. To deal with 1,600 trains per day, these boxes (and that at West London Junction) employed 25 signalmen and five booking boys.

Turning now to the Brighton side, there were boxes at each end of the station; as part of the 1895 widening the original North cabin had to be replaced by a new 58-lever box on the down side of the line, while the elevated South box above Falcon Junction was resited on to a similar gantry on the country side of the St John's Hill bridge, overlooking the road and equipped with 33 working levers. The station reconstruction of 1909-10 entailed another move for the North box, replaced on 5 June 1910 by a new 84 lever cabin slightly nearer to Victoria. The South box remained in situ but was provided with a new 38 lever frame; just below the box a double crossover linked the main and local lines. At this period the

LBSCR signalmen were handling 700-800 trains per day.

At Grouping the SR introduced alphabetical designations for the Clapham Junction boxes: the LSWR East became 'A', the LBSCR North 'B' and its South box 'C', the South Western main line West 'D' and the Windsor Line West 'E'. The LSWR pneumatic signalling had been modified for electro-pneumatic operation, but when the SR decided to instal colour light signalling on the lines out of Waterloo, it preferred to replace the existing frame in Clapham Junction 'A' box by a new 103-lever electric power frame (the same course was adopted for West London Junction box). 'E' box retained its EP frame for the time being as semaphore signalling was still in use on the Windsor Line west of Clapham Junction, but the small 'D' box in the cutting was abolished. These changes took place on 17 May 1936. As the pneumatic equipment in 'E' box required replacement, colour light signalling was extended along the Windsor Line to Point Pleasant Junction on 26 May 1940. Following the abolition of 'C' and 'D' boxes in 1952 and 1936 respectively, 'E' box became 'C', but from 2 November 1980 its functions were taken over by 'A' box.

In November 1946 the Southern Railway approved a scheme to instal colour light signalling on the Central section main lines, but it was not until 12 October 1952 that the new 103-lever Clapham Junction 'B' power box took over from the adjacent LBSCR mechanical cabin and from 'C' box at the other end of the station, both of which were then demolished.

This equipment had a short life. In 1976 the Southern Region embarked on the £35 million Victoria resignalling scheme to be controlled from a signalling centre at Pig Hill Clapham Junction on part of the site of the ex-LNWR Falcon Lane goods yard. The section of its Central division panel covering the Clapham Junction area was brought into use on 28 November 1980 and the 1952 'B' box was then closed, but the

building has been retained. Some track rationalisation was carried out; a ladder crossover to the east of the station replaced some of the crossings at Pouparts Junction and provided reversing facilities additional to the use of platforms 16 and 17. The double crossover in the cutting between St John's Hill and Boutflower Road bridges (a very wet spot) was abolished and another installed at New Wandsworth — in 1986 this also was replaced by a better located crossover at Balham.

Meanwhile, on the South Western side, the 1936 signalling was being controlled from the 1912 'A' box building. One change to the layout had been made during the autumn of 1947, when a double crossover between the main through and local lines had been provided in connection with major track formation renewal work in Clapham Cutting. During World War 2 a steel canopy had been erected over 'A' box to protect it from incendiary bombs and anti-aircraft shell fragments.

At 8.36am on 10 May 1965 the north end of the box suddenly dropped 4ft, fouling the Kensington and Windsor lines below. Part of a supporting girder had failed, and, as total collapse of the structure was feared, all traffic in and out of Waterloo was halted, creating chaos at the height of the rush hour. The Nine Elms crane was brought along to support the structure until its north end could be lifted on to steel trestles placed underneath, pending permanent repairs. It was found that severe corrosion of the girder had not been discovered during routine examination, while the steel canopy had added to the load

31

on the structure. West London Junction box proved to be in a similar dangerous state.

As platforms 1 and 2 were obstructed by the trestles, the Kensington trains were transferred to platforms 16 and 17 until these were required in September 1968 for terminating Central Division services. Meanwhile, the ex-LSWR gantry carrying the starting signals for platforms 1 to 4 had been demolished and shunting signals only were provided for departures from platforms 1 and 2 in the absence of any passenger trains; until the complete resignalling of 1990 Kensington departures were heralded only by a ground disc.

There were small fires beneath 'A' box on 30 December 1980 and 28 September 1985, briefly affecting services, but this ill-fated box suffered a more serious fire on Sunday 15 June 1986 which required the frame to be completely rewired. Normal operation of the Kensington and Longhedge lines and of the yard was not restored for some weeks. As the Waterloo Area Resignalling Scheme (WARS) was now under way, it was considered unnecessary to reconnect all existing facilities and the 1947 crossover between the through and local lines was left inoperative.

It was within the relay room of 'A' box that the fatal wiring errors were made which led to the Clapham Junction disaster of 12 December 1988. The subsequent investigation and the need to reinforce checking procedures, caused major delays and changes to the implementation of WARS. A plan to instal a temporary panel in 'A' box was abandoned, and control of the Clapham Junction area was transferred direct to the new Wimbledon signalling centre during the Spring Bank Holiday weekend of 26/27 May 1990, the severed connections thereupon being gradually restored.

A happier memory associated with 'A' box is its use by Terence Cuneo as the vantage point for his painting of Clapham Junction, which captures all the variety of traffic and motive power to be seen there in the early 1960s.

Of course, a busy centre like Clapham Junction has had its share of accidents. On the LSWR side, on 5 August 1874 an engine passed a ground signal at danger and emerged on to the up main line, where it was struck by an up train, injuring 35 passengers. A more destructive accident occurred on 20 August 1892 when the 9.50pm Waterloo to Feltham train (headed by Adams 4-4-2T No 374) over-ran signals and collided with an empty excursion train waiting to enter the yard — the guard of the empty train was killed and several of its carriages caught fire. Fog was a frequent hazard in South West London and on the night

Below:
The up loop platform 7 was electrified in 1967, but has only been used regularly since the Bournemouth semi-fast trains have been calling at Clapham Junction. Electro-diesels 73116 and Nos 73114, deputising for Class 442 stock, double head the 12.46 Poole to Waterloo out of platform 7 on 13 April 1989. *Author*

Right:
Signs of the recent fire in the buildings and footbridge above platforms 9 and 10 are visible in this picture of 4-SUB unit No 4658 passing with a down empty train on 26 July 1981. *C.J.Marsden*

of 22 January 1904 fog signal detonators had not been properly placed on the rails at Point Pleasant Junction, allowing the 9.30pm from Windsor to collide with the preceding 9.32pm from Kingston, standing at Clapham Junction West home signals. On 7 October 1908 six passengers and two staff were injured when the 6.30am Waterloo to Windsor struck a light engine which the East box signalman had assumed was clear of the running lines, although no bell signal had been given to confirm this.

Subsequent accidents involved electric trains: in dense fog at 10.26pm on 3 February 1921, the 9.30pm Waterloo to Kingston via Wimbledon (diverted via East Putney because of an earlier collision near Nine Elms) ran into the rear of the 9.36pm to Hounslow outside Clapham Junction. More recently, on 7 September 1972, the 14.05 Chessington to Waterloo started from the up local platform (No 10) against the signal and was derailed on the crossover leading to the through line. Then on 19 December 1975 the 08.59 Waterloo to Kingston was derailed between Clapham Junction and Wandsworth Town due to the premature removal of a component from a temporary facing crossover.

All these accidents were minor in comparison with the tragedy which took place on 12 December 1988, and whose details have been exhaustively covered in the media. Briefly, signal WF138 on the up through line in Clapham Cutting showed a false clear aspect,

allowing the 06.14 from Poole to collide with the 07.18 from Basingstoke, halted at the next signal while its driver was reporting the peculiar behaviour of signal WF138. A down empty stock train to Haslemere was also involved in the collision. Both up trains were crowded; 35 people lost their lives and large numbers were injured, 69 of them seriously.

Within a few hours the cause of the disaster had been traced to faults made during recent rewiring work inside 'A' box, which had made the track circuit controlling signal WF138 inoperative. Instead of the usual appointment of an Inspecting Officer to conduct the investigation, the Secretary of State for Transport ordered a public inquiry to be held, presided over by Anthony Hidden QC. This concentrated on the failures of supervision and management within the Southern Region, which had allowed unsafe working practices to develop. The inquiry's remit apparently did not extend to the delays at BRB and Department of Transport level which had caused the Waterloo resignalling scheme to be carried out as a matter of urgency, but with inadequate resources. The inquiry's report, published in November 1989, made 93 recommendations for improved equipment and procedures. Like the Armagh disaster a century earlier, Clapham (as the media has always referred to it) has focused attention on rail safety and the need to observe proper standards of work and to adopt the best modern technology.

Clapham Junction Station Platforms

	1900			1920			1950	
LSWR			**LSWR**			**S W Division**		
			1	(Kensington departures		1	Kensington departures	
2	Kensington departures			(Kensington arrivals		2	Kensington arrivals	
3	(Kensington arrivals		2	(Up Windsor local		3	Up Windsor local	
	(Up Windsor			(Up Windsor through		4	Up Windsor through	
4	Down Windsor		3	(Down Windsor through		5	Down Windsor through	
				(Down Windsor local		6	Down Windsor local	
			4	(Up main loop		7	Up main loop	
				(Up main local		8	Up main through	
5	(Up main local		5	(Up main through		9	Down main through	
	(Up main through			(Down main through		10	Up main local	
6	Down main		6	Down main local		11	Down main local	
LBSCR			**LBSCR**			**Central Division**		
6	Up main		7	Up main		12	Up through	
7	Up local		8	Down main		13	Down through	
8	(Down main		9	Up local		14	Up local	
	(Down local		10	Down local		15	Down local	
9	(WLER departures		11	WLER departures		16	Kensington departures	
	(WLER arrivals		12	WLER arrivals		17	Kensington arrivals	

Notes

From 1968 platform 16 has been used for up trains terminating at Clapham Junction which. then return from
platform 17. Platform 1 was taken out of use from 13 April 1980 and Kensington trains arrive and depart at
platform 2.

Prior to 1876 the LSWR Kensington platforms were numbered 1 and 2 and the then separate Windsor Line
platforms 3 and 4.

The Passing Scene — Saturday 25 February 1939

Time (pm)	Train	Loco	Class	Duty (SR)
2.43	Up milk train (Windsor Line)	458	T14 4-6-0	35
2.55	Vans ex Stewarts Lane (to Windsor line)	1602	T 0-6-0T	78
2.58	11.30am Weymouth-Waterloo	784	N15 4-6-0	383
3.00	Light Waterloo (Windsor line) to sidings	1798	U 2-6-0	36
3.01	2.54 Waterloo-Salisbury	2333	N15X 4-6-0	1
3.05	Empty coaches Waterloo to yard	322	M7 0-4-4T	75
3.07	3.00 Waterloo-Ilfracombe	456	N15 4-6-0	445
3.10	Battersea-Norwood freight	1815	N 2-6-0	745
3.12	Down light engine (Central)	2553	C2X 0-6-0	516
3.30	1.3 Salisbury-Waterloo	486	H15 4-6-0	4
3.30	Empty coaches Waterloo to yard	241	M7 0-4-4T	77
3.35	2.12 Tunbridge Wells-Victoria	2007	I1X 4-4-2T	600
3.37	3.30 Waterloo-Bournemouth West	778	N15 4-6-0	59
3.40	10.40 Manchester-Hastings	416	L12 4-4-0	
3.40	10.30 Ilfracombe-Waterloo ('ACE')	864	LN 4-6-0	7
3.45	Nine Elms-Feltham freight	167	L11 4-4-0	
3.50	Empty coaches yard to Waterloo	740	N15 4-6-0	2
3.55	Norwood-Battersea freight	1911	W 2-6-4T	
4.01	3.54 Waterloo-Basingstoke	465	D15 4-4-0	282
4.02	1.00 Bournemouth West-Waterloo	933	V 4-4-0	385
4.02	3.55 Victoria-Uckfield-Brighton	2054	B4 4-4-0	669
4.10	Acton-Norwood freight	8754	57XX 0-6-0T	GWR
4.11	Norwood-Willesden Junction freight	1919	W 2-6-4T	565
4.20	Brent-Battersea freight	3261	3F 0-6-0	LMS
4.22	Down light engine (Central)	1712	C 0-6-0	517
4.22	12.35 Bournemouth West-Waterloo	447	T14 4-6-0	37
4.25	Up light engine (Central)	1815	N 2-6-0	745
4.37	4.30 Waterloo-Weymouth	926	V 4-4-0	386
4.47	3.27 Forest Row-Victoria	2001	I1X 4-4-2T	605
4.50	1.35 Weymouth-Waterloo	931	V 4-4-0	384
4.50	Willesden-Clapham Junction parcels	7710	2F 0-6-2T	LMS
4.52	4.45 Waterloo-Bournemouth West	932	V 4-4-0	387
4.53	2.55 Salisbury-Waterloo	1807	U 2-6-0	268
4.57	4.50 Victoria-Uckfield-Brighton	2067	B4X 4-4-0	667
5.05	Ferme Park-Feltham freight	4570	N1 0-6-2T	LNER
5.07	5.00 Waterloo-Yeovil Junction	740	N15 4-6-0	2
5.07	Up light engine (Windsor Line)	469	D15 4-4-0	
5.14	5.09 Victoria-East Grinstead	2078	I3 4-4-2T	536
5.20	Gatwick-Victoria race special	1905	U1 2-6-0	spl
5.26	Gatwick-Victoria Pullman special	793	N15 4-6-0	spl
5.27	Southampton-Waterloo flying boat special	472	D15 4-4-0	spl

Throughout the afternoon carriage shunting in the yard was performed by '02' 0-4-4Ts Nos 179 (duty 83) and 212 (duty 85). 'M7' 0-4-4T No 357 (duty 69) also assisted with shunting.

Chelsea FC was playing at home and an augmented service of trains was provided from Clapham Junction to Chelsea & Fulham station and thence to Kensington Addison Road. The following locos were noted on these trains: 'M7' 0-4-4Ts Nos 38, 40, 249 (duty 65), 323, 673 (duty 70); '02' 0-4-4T No 204 and 'R' class 0-4-4T No 1667.

2 The South West Lines

The opening of the London & Southampton Railway from Nine Elms to Woking on 21 May 1838 provided five trains each way on weekdays and four on Sundays, all of them serving Wandsworth as well as the two other stations within the London area at Wimbledon and Kingston (which became Surbiton in 1867). Fares to Wandsworth were 1s (1 shilling or 5p) first class and 6d (6 pence or 2½p) second class. When the line was extended westward, successively to Winchfield, then Basingstoke and finally in May 1840 to Southampton, fast trains which did not call at Wandsworth were added to the timetable. In the September 1845 time bill, seven of the 16 departures from Nine Elms were fast to Kingston, Woking or Basingstoke; the stopping trains which served Wandsworth were mostly bound for Guildford (to which a branch had been opened in May 1845), plus the two Southampton slow trains, including the 'Parliamentary' by which passengers to Wandsworth were conveyed for 3d (1p). A reduced first class fare of 8d (3p) was available on the 9.00am from Nine Elms, while day return tickets were issued at 1s 4d (7p) first class and 8d (3p) second.

The Richmond Railway, opened on 27 July 1846, was intended to cater for suburban traffic with a frequent service, and of its 17 weekday trains from Nine Elms in February 1848, all but two served its Wandsworth station. On Sundays 11 trains ran to Richmond, with a three hour gap during the morning to enable public and staff to attend church. The other original stations on this line were at Putney, Barnes and Mortlake. The Richmond Railway was worked by the LSWR and was absorbed by it at the end of 1846. The main line station, then named Clapham Common, was less well served with only nine trains stopping on weekdays, though a similar number passed through non stop. Fares from Nine Elms to both stations were identical, except that third class travellers were charged a penny extra for the slightly longer distance to Wandsworth. First class fares had been reduced to 8d (3p) single and 10d (4p) day return.

The Metropolitan Extension to Waterloo was opened on 11 July 1848 with an intermediate station at Vauxhall, whereupon the original terminus at Nine Elms was closed to passenger traffic. The Richmond branch was continued to the west by the Windsor, Staines & South Western Railway, which opened as far as Datchet on 22 August 1848 and reached Windsor on 1 December 1849. The new line had its own station at Richmond (the original terminus remained open for local trains until September 1849), before crossing the Thames into Middlesex to serve Twickenham and Feltham. This company also built an alternative route (now known as the Hounslow Loop) from Barnes to rejoin the Windsor line at Feltham Junction. This was opened to Smallberry Green, near Isleworth, on 22 August 1849 and throughout on 1 February 1850. Original stations were at Chiswick, Kew (later Kew Bridge), Brentford, Isleworth and Hounslow. The WS&SW company was absorbed by the LSWR from 30 June 1850. The Windsor Line was extended from Staines to Ascot on 4 June 1856 and to Wokingham and over the SER to Reading a month later.

On the main line an additional station had been built at Malden in December 1846; after numerous changes in its name this finally became New Malden in 1957. A short branch was opened on 1 February 1849 to a small terminus at Hampton Court, on the Surrey bank of the Thames opposite the palace. An intermediate station on the branch at Thames Ditton was added in November 1851. Hampton Court became the destination of most of the stopping trains which served Clapham Common, with eight weekday services in 1857; in addition four main line trains called — three for Alton via Guildford and the Southampton 'Parliamentary' slow. Fifteen trains passed through without stopping, including two fasts to Hampton Court and one to the Chertsey branch, opened in February 1848. On Sundays, 14 of the 18 departures from Waterloo called at Clapham Common.

In 1857 Wandsworth was served by 15 trains from Waterloo at approximately hourly intervals, many of them combined services for Twickenham and Hounslow which divided at Barnes. The 14 non-stopping trains were mostly bound for Windsor and beyond. Riverside attractions brought out the crowds on summer Sundays and the LSWR provided a generous service of 34 trains, of which 21 called at Wandsworth.

Right:
**Rebuilt Beattie 'Vesuvius' class 2-4-0
No 18 approaches Clapham Junction
on a down Portsmouth line train
c1890.**
Ian Allan Library — L&GRP

There were frequent morning departures from Waterloo before the church interval was imposed at 11.00am, and provision was made in the working timetable for extra return trains from Twickenham and Hounslow during the evening.

The decade from 1859 saw considerable expansion of the LSWR's suburban system. On 4 April 1859 the Wimbledon & Dorking Railway was opened from Wimbledon or West Barnes Junction (the present Raynes Park) through stations at Old Malden & Worcester Park and Ewell to Epsom, where it joined the LBSCR to continue as a joint line to Leatherhead. The local company, always worked by the LSWR, was absorbed by it in 1862. The Leatherhead trains swelled the 1861 service at Clapham Common to 21 on weekdays and 16 on Sundays. However, Wandsworth continued to do better with 25 weekday trains from Waterloo. From 3 August 1860 the Windsor Line had separate platforms at Waterloo and its own pair of tracks all the way from the terminus to the divergence from the main line at Falcon Junction.

When Clapham Junction station opened in March 1863, it was served on weekdays by 20 of the 43 Main line departures from Waterloo — 15 for Hampton Court or Leatherhead and five for main line destinations. On the Windsor Line, only 15 out of 40 trains called at the new station, and several of these managed to coincide with main line departures (a practice which still persists).

Kingston, which had spurned the London & Southampton Railway, was belatedly reached on 1 July 1863 by a branch from Twickenham, with intermediate stations at Teddington and Hampton Wick. In addition to trains from Waterloo, Kingston was served by North London Railway services to the City, using two curves opened on 1 February 1862, from Kew East Junction to New Kew Junction on the Hounslow Loop, and from Chiswick Junction on that line to Mortlake Junction on the Barnes-Richmond section of the Windsor Line.

An independent company, the Thames Valley Railway, had promoted the single line branch to Shepperton which opened on 1 November 1864. This left the Kingston line at Thames Valley Junction (known as Strawberry Hill after a station was provided in 1873) and had intermediate stations at Fulwell, Hampton and Sunbury. In 1867, nine trains served the branch on weekdays, but third class passengers could only travel by the 7.25am or the 8.20pm from Waterloo. The TVR company was fully absorbed by the LSWR in 1867. With the opening on 3 April 1866 of the LCDR/LSWR line from Longhedge Junction to Clapham Junction, five trains on weekdays ran from Kingston or Twickenham to Ludgate Hill.

Traffic at Clapham Junction was growing: by April 1867 the station was being served by 37 weekday trains from Waterloo via the Windsor Line, while 14 more (mainly for Windsor and Shepperton) passed through without stopping. Even on Sundays there were 26 trains calling. However the main line service was less frequent, with 23 of Waterloo's 42 weekday

Top right:
**Drummond 'E10' class 4-2-2-0 No 369 with a down
Bournemouth express in Clapham Cutting; the difference in
level of the local lines is noticeable here, c1910.**
Ian Allan Library — H.Gordon Tidey

Above right:
**A down West of England restaurant car express headed by
Drummond 'L12' 4-4-0 No 419 passes Clapham Cutting
intermediate box, c1910.**
Ian Allan Library — Bucknall collection

Right:
**The unique superheated 'M7' 0-4-4T No 126 works a down
race special through Clapham Cutting, c1920. The rear
vehicles are one of the sets of elliptical roofed six-wheelers
built about 1904 for excursion and special traffic.**
Ian Allan Library — Locomotive Publishing Company (LPC)

departures stopping at the station — only two of these trains (for Alton and Godalming respectively) had destinations beyond Woking. On Sundays 15 trains called and three passed through. The 1860s saw the influx of the Beattie 2-4-0 well tanks on to the suburban services, where they remained in charge for the next 20 years.

A momentous day for the LSWR in the London area was 1 January 1869. On that day, Kingston, which had been served only by the circuitous branch from Twickenham, was provided with a direct link to the main line at Malden. This used a new high level station at Kingston, adjacent to the original terminus, and had an intermediate station at Norbiton. Between there and Malden the new line burrowed under the main line and ran as an independent pair of tracks on the down side as far as the east end of Wimbledon station. The Epsom and Leatherhead line at West Barnes Junction was altered to join the new tracks instead of the main line itself and a station named Raynes Park was provided there on 30 October 1871 on the Epsom and Kingston lines. It was the intention that the Kingston trains would run from Wimbledon to Ludgate Hill via the LSWR/LBSCR joint lines and thence over the LCDR, thus replacing the through service via Richmond and Clapham Junction. Kingston travellers, however, preferred to go to Waterloo, and

gradually most trains to and from Ludgate Hill ran only as far as Wimbledon.

The same day also saw the opening of the line from Kensington Addison Road via Hammersmith and Brentford Road (Gunnersbury from 1871) to a new terminal station at Richmond. From Gunnersbury, a spur, which enjoyed a passenger service from June 1870, joined the Hounslow Loop east of Kew Bridge. Another short link from Gunnersbury to the N&SWJ line at South Acton enabled the North London service to Richmond to be diverted over the new line, replacing the indirect route via the Kew East to New Kew and Chiswick Junction to Mortlake Junction curves — the latter was then taken out of use. From 1 June 1877 the Metropolitan District Railway was linked to these lines at Studland Road Junction, Hammersmith, and commenced to run its trains through to Richmond and other destinations.

Between 1875 and 1877 a pair of goods lines was built on the north side of the Windsor Line from Nine Elms to Clapham Junction, joining the Longhedge Junction line at Ludgate Junction and connecting there with the realigned tracks through the station. After inspecting this work on 31 December 1876, Colonel Yolland remarked that "Clapham Junction is a very busy place, on an ordinary weekday 656 trains are signalled forward from the East box and on Derby Day 1023 trains' — a surprising comment as the Derby was then mainly a Brighton occasion, but that company had the reputation of charging racegoers the maximum the traffic would bear. Even after the LBSCR line to Epsom was opened in 1847, punters were still prepared to take LSWR specials to Kingston (Surbiton) and walk the rest of the way to Epsom Downs.

Below:
Adams 'Jubilee' 0-4-2 No 655 passes Clapham Junction with a bogie block set on a train for Guildford via Cobham, c1920. In the foreground some of the complicated LBSCR overhead wiring is visible.
Ian Allan Library — H.C.Casserley

The LSWR enjoyed its own lucrative race traffic. Ascot Week always saw the Windsor Line at its busiest, and when a new course at Kempton Park was opened, a station alongside was provided on 18 July 1878 and the Shepperton branch was doubled at the same time.

On the Windsor Line a new station was opened at St. Margarets, between Richmond and Twickenham, on 2 October 1876, and another at Queens Road Battersea on 1 November 1877. There the pair of goods lines was upgraded to passenger status during 1896-97 and designated as the Windsor local lines,

Above:
The down 'Atlantic Coast Express' approaches Earlsfield behind 'King Arthur' 4-6-0 No E452 *Sir Meliagrance*, c1930. *Ian Allan Library — Real Photos*

Below:
A down semi-fast train formed of SECR and LSWR non-corridor stock in Clapham Cutting. The headcode is for the Bournemouth direction, but the loco is a new 'U1' 2-6-0, A899, carrying a duty number belonging to its home shed of Fratton, c1931. *Ian Allan Library — E.R.Wethersett*

Above:
'Lord Nelson' 4-6-0 No 865 *Sir John Hawkins* **is seen c1935, on a down West of England express in Clapham Cutting.**
Ian Allan Library — LPC

although they did not serve Queens Road station, which had to wait until 1 October 1909 to be provided with an up local line platform. In 1980 this station was renamed Queenstown Road, many years after the thoroughfare had changed its name. During 1877-78 the lines into Waterloo had been diverted at Nine Elms on to a new viaduct and the terminus itself was enlarged on 16 December 1878 by the two platform South station, intended to handle suburban traffic to the Epsom, Kingston and Hampton Court lines.

The 1880s was another period of suburban expansion. The first addition on 1 January 1883 was a short curve from Hounslow Junction to Whitton Junction, which enabled the Gunnersbury-Hounslow service to be extended to Twickenham, and later for the Hounslow Loop to be worked as a circular route. At Twickenham, on 22 October 1883, the line from Kingston was carried over the Windsor lines by the first of the flyovers built by the LSWR to avoid the delays of flat junctions.

In order to counter a scheme supported by the Metropolitan District for a line from Putney via Kingston and Surbiton to Guildford, the LSWR promoted its own line from Hampton Court Junction to Guildford via Cobham, with a connecting line from Leatherhead to Effingham Junction. These sections were opened on 2 February 1885. The remainder of the original proposed route, from Putney to Surbiton, was to be built jointly by the LSWR and the MDR, but as the latter was unable to raise its share of the capital, the LSWR adopted an alternative plan for its own line from Putney Bridge (then the MDR terminus) to Wimbledon. This had stations at East Putney, Southfields and Wimbledon Park, and ran into two terminal platforms on the north side at Wimbledon. District trains commenced running to Wimbledon on 3 June 1889 and were joined by a LSWR service from

Waterloo on 1 July, via a steeply-graded spur from the Windsor Line at Point Pleasant Junction, Wandsworth, to East Putney.

Increasing traffic as well as the new branches made it necessary to quadruple sections of both main and Windsor lines. Between the west end of Clapham Junction and Wimbledon additional local lines were provided; the up side was brought into use on 30 March 1883 and the down on 2 March 1884. Originally through Clapham Cutting the new lines were at a higher level than the existing tracks, which became the through lines, but the differential has been reduced over the years by re-ballasting. Widening here was followed by the opening of a new station on 1 April 1884 in Garratt Lane, given the more attractive name of Earlsfield & Summerstown. Platforms on the through lines were not provided until 1897.

Meanwhile, Wimbledon station had been rebuilt and partly resited in 1881. Between Wimbledon East and Malden the existing independent Kingston lines were now incorporated in the new arrangement of four tracks in parallel. At Raynes Park the up Epsom line was brought under the main line by a dive-under on 16 March 1884, and the station was rebuilt with two island platforms serving the main local and Epsom lines. At Malden the 1869 underbridge for the Kingston lines continued to serve as a dive-under for the down line, and a new spur was built in March 1884 to bring the up Kingston track to join the main line on the up side.

Between Malden and Hampton Court Junction, additional local lines were added on each side,

except through Surbiton station where the widening was made on the down side, leaving the 1840 building intact for a further 50 years. The section from Malden to the east end of Surbiton cutting was completed in 1882 and the more difficult stretch through the cutting and station on to Hampton Court Junction a year later.

On the Windsor Line, quadrupling took place from the west end of Clapham Junction to Barnes Junction between 1885 and 1887, involving the rebuilding of Wandsworth and Putney stations. The 1889 up line spur from East Putney crossed the Windsor lines by a lofty viaduct before joining them at Point Pleasant Junction. The LSWR station at Wandsworth was given the suffix 'Town' in 1903, probably to distinguish it from the LBSCR's Wandsworth Common and Wandsworth Road.

On 1 July 1894, a curve was opened from Shacklegate Junction, Teddington, to Fulwell Junction, largely to enable Kempton Park race trains to run via Kingston as well as via Richmond; it was not used by regular services until June 1901 and then only once a day. Another popular racecourse was Hurst Park, to the west of Hampton Court, where the station was rebuilt and enlarged in 1899. On Bank Holidays the races, the fair, the palace and the river would bring as many as 50 special trains on to the branch.

This quadrupling of the lines through the suburbs only accentuated the congestion on the approaches to Waterloo. Therefore, during 1885, a new North station was opened to cater for Windsor Line traffic, followed in 1891 by the first widening of the Metropolitan Extension since it was built in 1848. Two additional lines were provided between Waterloo and Vauxhall — a second down Windsor and a second up main (both termed local lines). Vauxhall station was extensively rebuilt and was provided with two up platforms on the Windsor side to match the two on

the main line — all Waterloo-bound trains at that time stopped at Vauxhall for tickets to be collected.

By the summer of 1890 there were 100 weekday departures from Waterloo on the Windsor Line, of which 86 served Clapham Junction — most of the non-stopping trains ran during the evening rush hour. On Sundays all of the 54 trains on the Windsor Line called at Clapham Junction. The service to the main line platform was still inferior to that on the Windsor Line; on weekdays 78 trains called, while 10 locals and 19 long distance ones passed through, but the station now enjoyed several semi-fast services to Alton and Basingstoke. On Sundays 34 main line trains stopped at Clapham.

During the 1880s the Adams 'Radial' 4-4-2Ts had taken over the London suburban services, many of them being stationed at a new engine shed at Fulwell opened in May 1897. From 1899 much of the suburban rolling stock was stabled in sidings built between the main and East Putney lines at Wimbledon Park, with an exit on to the up main lines at Merton Road box (this road has since been renamed Durnsford Road). Another improvement, completed on 26 November 1899 was an additional up line between Twickenham and St Margarets.

However, there was still only one down main line track all the way from Waterloo to beyond Clapham Junction and only one up line from the east end of that station to Wandsworth Road box outside Vauxhall. The Windsor Line had three tracks from Waterloo to Vauxhall, two thence to Queens Road East and four from there to Ludgate Junction, with quadruple line recommencing at Clapham Junction West box. The four tracks between Queens Road and Ludgate Junction were arranged alternately (a relic of their original goods and passenger use) and did not correspond to the parallel arrangement of quadruple tracks elsewhere.

Clapham Junction station was therefore a bottleneck on both lines, limiting any increase in train services: on the main line it was not unusual to run combined trains out of Waterloo, splitting at Surbiton, for example, into portions for the main and New Guildford via Cobham lines, sometimes double-headed as far as Surbiton. The answer to this problem, the eight year task of widening and rebuilding Clapham Junction station, has already been described in the preceding chapter. One of the constraints on widening the main lines between Clapham Junction and Queens Road was the presence of the LBSCR tracks alongside, so that expansion could only take place northwards on the Windsor Line side. Inwards of Vauxhall the area was heavily built up, and before the viaduct could be widened the inhabitants had to be rehoused in tenement blocks erected by the LSWR.

A short length of the new down local line outside Waterloo was completed in July 1900, to be followed by a long section from Wandsworth Road to West London Junction on 27 October 1901, which was extended back to Vauxhall West from 5 July 1903. The gap between Waterloo 'B' box and Vauxhall

West, including a new down platform at Vauxhall, was filled on 1 April 1906, and finally the down local road was extended from West London Junction to Clapham Junction East on 9 June 1907.

Widening the up main line depended on space being found by shifting the Windsor Line tracks northwards; in March 1906, West London Junction box had to be moved bodily aside (it was soon replaced by an overhead pneumatic cabin in February 1912). The first section of the additional up local line between Nine Elms Loco Junction and Wandsworth Road came into use on 11 August 1907. After the Windsor Lines and the West London sidings had been realigned, the stretch from Clapham Junction East to Queens Road followed on 4 October 1908, and finally that from Queens Road to Loco Junction on 20 December, completing quadruple track throughout between Waterloo and Worting Junction. A fifth road, the up relief, was provided between Waterloo 'C' box and the terminus on 24 January 1909, when the first three platforms of the rebuilt station opened.

The Windsor Line tracks between Queens Road and Ludgate Junction were altered to the parallel arrangement on 13 October 1907 as part of the final stage in the rebuilding of Clapham Junction station. This change involved the down Windsor local line through Queens Road station becoming once again a goods line for departures from Nine Elms yard. Plans for electrification required the provision of two extra Windsor Line tracks between Wandsworth Road and Loco Junction. This was done by widening the viaduct on the main line side, where land had become available following the removal of the locomotive works to Eastleigh, and slewing tracks successively to provide the new down Windsor line on 16 January 1916 and the up road a week later. The up Windsor local line was extended from Queens Road East to Loco Junction on 1 December 1918 when a new overhead cabin replaced the existing box and that at Wandsworth Road. Plans for further rearrange-

Below:
The Brookwood Necropolis train, headed by a 'M7' 0-4-4T, passes Wimbledon Park sidings in 1902. The East Putney line curves in from the left beyond the signal gantry; suburban stock in the sidings in the background is arc-roofed and mainly six-wheel. *Lens of Sutton*

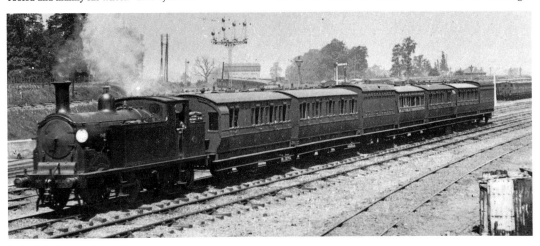

Above:
Wimbledon Park sidings on 20 November 1951. An up suburban train formed of an augmented 4-SUB unit of LSWR origin climbs the Durnsford Road flyover, while a postwar steel bodied 4-SUB unit passes with a down Kingston Roundabout train. In the distance, Durnsford Road power station is steaming hard to generate the current for these and other trains. *Ian Allan Library — British Rail*

ment here were never carried out and the one down line through Queenstown Road station remains a witness to the non-fulfilment of the LSWR's aim to have eight tracks between Waterloo and Clapham Junction.

To signal these 3 miles 76 chains there were boxes at Waterloo 'A', 'B', and 'C', Vauxhall East and West, Loco Junction, Queens Road East and West, West London Junction and Clapham Junction 'A'. In LSWR days, elderly signalmen working in this busy area were able to transfer to quieter suburban or country boxes without losing their pension entitlements.

With the worst of the bottlenecks removed, the eve of World War 1 saw 130 weekday departures from Waterloo for the Windsor Line, 103 of them serving Clapham Junction. On the main line side there were 174 departures, of which 105 stopped at Clapham Junction. Most main line stopping trains to Woking served the station as well as several semi-fasts for places further afield. On Sundays some of the subur-

ban routes ran to regular interval timings, with extra trains during the summer to serve the riverside resorts. (The LSWR had abandoned the Sunday morning church interval in 1901.)

From 1898 onwards, the Drummond 'M7' class 0-4-4Ts began to work the local services out of Waterloo, sharing the longer distance duties with 'K10' and 'L11' 4-4-0s. However, some Adams 4-4-2Ts still remained in the London area until the early 1920s.

Left:
'Merchant Navy' Pacific No 35028 (then un-named) leans to the curve through Clapham Junction with the 6.30pm Waterloo to Weymouth express, on 27 June 1949.
Ian Allan Library — C. C. B.Herbert

Simultaneously, the old rolling stock on the suburban trains was replaced by new four-coach close-coupled Bogie Block sets, built in such quantity that by 1914 non-bogie carriages had become a rarity at Waterloo.

Despite these improvements, the LSWR was now facing serious competition from the tramcar, the motorbus, and the District electric trains which from 1905 had been running over South Western tracks to Richmond and Wimbledon. The company decided late in 1912 to embark on its own £1.1 million electrification scheme covering 47 miles of inner suburban routes, with the prospect of a second stage to extend electric traction as far as Guildford. The 600-volt dc third rail system was chosen as this would be compatible with the third and fourth rail MDR electrification to Wimbledon already in existence. Power was to be generated from the company's own 25,000kW station at Durnsford Road, Wimbledon, where rolling stock maintenance and stabling facilities would be provided. With the economy typical of Herbert Walker's management, the three-car electric units were to be converted from the relatively new four coach bogie block sets, losing their second class accommodation in the process.

Below:
Urie 'H15' 4-6-0 30483 traverses the 1947 crossovers approaching the station on 14 March 1952 with the 12.54pm Waterloo-Basingstoke. *Ian Allan Library — R.E.Vincent*

The original timetable for electrification was delayed by the outbreak of World War 1 and the needs of the war effort. Electric trains began public services between Waterloo and Wimbledon via East Putney on 25 October 1915, followed by the major conversion of the Kingston Roundabout and Shepperton lines on 30 January 1916, the Hounslow Loop from 12 March, Hampton Court from 18 June, and finally a short length of stage two to Claygate on 20 November 1916.

Two changes were made to the existing pattern of services. The Hounslow Loop was operated as a circular route and for the succeeding 70 years only infrequent trains ran direct from Hounslow to Feltham. The Shepperton service was transferred from the Richmond route to run via Kingston, with only a few rush-hour trains remaining via Richmond. The suburban services which had generally run at approximately hourly intervals with steam traction were now operating every 10 minutes to Kingston and every 15 minutes to Hampton Court, with half-hourly trains on other routes. Between 1915 and 1920 annual passenger numbers increased from 23 million to 52 million, resulting in serious overcrowding. To alleviate this, the Claygate electric service was withdrawn in June 1919 and further bogie block coaches were converted into two-coach trailer sets to be coupled between the electric units during the peak hours. Weekday suburban departures from Waterloo increased from 250 in 1914 to 461 (plus 54 main line

trains) in 1922, the year when the rebuilding of the terminus was finally completed.

To conform to the regular interval pattern of the electric services, the remaining steam suburban trains (to Windsor, Reading, Leatherhead and Guildford) also ran to standard timings which omitted stops at Clapham Junction. With such frequent electric services running, passengers for the outer suburbs could easily change at Wimbledon, Surbiton or Richmond, where the steam trains made their first stop. The postwar reorganisation of long distance services on a regular interval basis also eliminated the occasional stops made by them at Clapham Junction; there only remained a few calls by up trains (such as the 5.15pm from Salisbury) to detach milk vans or tank wagons in the up loop. Not all the electric trains stopped at Clapham Junction — the Windsor Line services worked on a skip-stop pattern, and the rush-hour extras to Shepperton were fast to Mortlake or Richmond, while Wandsworth Town was the first stop for peak-hour Hounslow and East Putney line trains.

Eventually, in 1925, the Southern Railway carried out part of the LSWR's postponed second stage of electrification. On 12 July electric traction was extended from Hampton Court Junction to Guildford via Cobham, from Raynes Park to Epsom, Leatherhead and Effingham Junction and over former LBSCR metals to Dorking North. Further three-car units sup-

Above:

In unpromising weather for a railtour, 'Schools' No 30932 *Blundells* passes Clapham Junction with the Ian Allan excursion to the Somerset & Dorset line on 25 April 1954.
Brian Morrison

plied by outside builders were a modified version of the original LSWR stock, still retaining the characteristic torpedo ends. The standard suburban service frequency became 20 minutes — Sir Herbert Walker felt that casual travellers would not be willing to wait longer. On the extensions, Epsom line trains stopped at all stations, but weekday New Guildford services were fast to Surbiton. Electrification was later extended to Staines and Windsor on 6 July 1930, trains usually running non-stop to Richmond.

As each conversion was made, there was an immediate growth in traffic stimulated by effective SR publicity linked to the activities of speculative housebuilders. The LSWR electrification had only involved one additional station at Barnes Bridge, opened on 12 March 1916, but the SR built new stations within the inner suburban area at: Motspur Park (1925), North Sheen and Whitton (both in 1930), Syon Lane (1931), Stoneleigh (1932) and Berrylands (1933).

Inevitably, rush-hour trains became more and more crowded, especially on the Epsom line, and services

could not be increased because all up local trains had to cross the path of both up and down main line trains outside Waterloo to reach their platforms (1 to 4). The LSWR had failed to grasp this problem in 1914, but the SR found the solution by taking the up local line over the through roads by a flyover near Durnsford Road, Wimbledon, and rearranging the tracks thence into Waterloo into through and local line pairs. In addition, colour light signalling was provided between Waterloo and Hampton Court Junction, automatic operation replacing small section boxes such as Clapham Cutting and Earlsfield. Elsewhere, the new lever frames were installed in the existing boxes. Rearrangement of the tracks and the inauguration of colour light signalling between Vauxhall and Malden was carried out during a six-hour period on 17 May 1936 — a feat which appears incredible today. Resignalling was completed by new boxes at Surbiton and Hampton Court Junction in June, and finally by a 309-lever power box at Waterloo (replacing six manual boxes) brought into operation during a 55-minute interruption of the service on 18 October 1936.

At last services could be improved. Stopping trains were added on the Epsom line enabling those to Dorking and Effingham Junction to run non-stop to Wimbledon or Motspur Park, where a new branch was opened to Tolworth on 29 May 1938 and to Chessington South on 28 May 1939. Main line electrification was carried out in stages during 1937 to Farnham, Guildford, Alton and Portsmouth. On the Windsor Line electric traction reached Chertsey in January 1937 and Reading in January 1939 — the last extension on the South Western lines for 28 years. As a consequence of the 1937 electrifications, steam stock was no longer stabled at Wimbledon Park sidings, which had been in partial use by electric trains since 1917. Likewise the former steam loco shed at Fulwell was transformed into Strawberry Hill electric depot between 1916 and 1923.

Besides adding new stations, the Southern Railway rebuilt some of the more important ones within the suburban area: Wimbledon, in 1929 in conjunction with the opening of the new line to Sutton; Epsom, also in 1929, where a new station at the junction of the LSWR and LBSCR routes replaced two separate stations; Kingston, in 1935, where the old low level terminus was demolished and a bay added to the high level; Surbiton, in 1937, providing an additional down through line; and Richmond, in 1938, combining the terminal station for District and North London trains with the SR through platforms and also incorporating an area of colour light signalling controlled from a new 'glasshouse' style box. The outbreak of World War 2 interrupted similar plans for rebuilding at Twickenham, which was carried out on a more modest scale in 1954.

Wartime conditions brought a drastic contraction of suburban services. Although the SR tried to maintain rush hour commuter trains, outside the peaks most individual branches were reduced to an hourly frequency and during the period of nightly bombing some lines ran as local shuttle services in the evening. Main line traffic serving the military centres of South West England was heavy, and in 1943 the SR, eager to demonstrate its new 'Merchant Navy' Pacifics' contribution to the war effort, arranged for the usual two portions of the wartime version of the 'Atlantic Coast Express' to be combined into one 16-coach train. As this would have blocked the tracks outside Waterloo, the up train stopped at Clapham Junction to detach the rear carriages, which were worked into the terminus by a 'M7' tank.

Recovery from the reduced services and slower schedules of the war years was protracted and the prewar 20-minute suburban frequency was not restored until the autumn of 1948. Gradually the old three-car electric units and two-car trailer sets were re-formed into four-car units, the process being accelerated after 1945 by the delivery of the all steel 4-SUB units. These were followed from 1952 by the similar 4-EPB units until the last of the prewar wooden-bodied stock had gone by 1962.

During the 'austerity' years few major works were carried out. In 1948 a new Wimbledon 'A' box replaced the 1899 LSWR structure. On the Windsor Line, colour light signalling had been installed in May 1940 from Clapham Junction to Point Pleasant Junction, with an 'ARP' pattern box there. Following the serious 1955 collision at Barnes, this was extended through Putney to Mortlake in February 1959, controlled from a new power box at Barnes. Another essential task during the 1950s was the conversion of the SR's power supply to the national grid network, transformed into 600 volts dc via unmanned rectifier sub-stations in place of the life-expired rotary converters. The LSWR's Durnsford Road generating plant was therefore shut down in 1958 and was demolished in 1965, its site and that of the adjacent LSWR car sheds being occupied in 1974 by the new East Wimbledon depot which maintains the South Western Lines' electric rolling stock.

In the autumn of 1958, the BR financial situation required urgent economies, and the SR's contribution was to reduce the standard suburban frequency from 20 to 30 minutes. Epsom line trains now began to call at Clapham Junction, although this route still enjoyed three trains per hour until 1963. The reductions still left Kingston with four trains hourly — two to Shepperton and two around the Roundabout.

The new timetable which accompanied the end of steam traction, on 10 July 1967, provided an improved 15-minute peak hour service to the Chessington and Hampton Court lines and extra short workings to Strawberry Hill via Kingston. Fast commuter trains to Dorking and Effingham Junction, which had hitherto taken the through line out to Raynes Park, were now scheduled to share the local line with the stopping services.

In 1976, Sunday services, which had followed closely the weekday pattern since 1967, were reduced drastically, though the worst cuts were later restored. May 1985 saw the long-established Kingston Roundabout service cut short outside the peak hours to a Waterloo (WL) to Kingston via Richmond working. Similarly, the off-peak Hounslow Loop trains had their return circular route cut short at Twickenham, but from May 1986 were instead diverted from Hounslow Junction to run to Weybridge or Woking and later to Guildford.

Though inner suburban services had been reduced, other types of trains were now stopping at Clapham Junction. Back in June 1951, off-peak trains to Windsor and Weybridge began to call, joined in May 1979 by most services for the Reading and Camberley lines. The curtailment of the Kingston Roundabout service in May 1985 enabled paths on the slow lines to be found for stopping trains to Guildford via the main line and via Cobham, which then served Clapham Junction. The hourly combined Basingstoke and Alton trains also called at the station on the fast line. A year later, in May 1986, the semi-fast trains to Bournemouth began to stop, followed in May 1988 by the diesel-hauled Salisbury semi-fasts every two hours and the alternate hourly Southampton and Farnham train. Finally in May 1989 the semi-fast services to Portsmouth Harbour gained a Clapham Junction stop, so that during the off-peak period the only South Western trains passing through were the fast 'Network Expresses'.

During these years, South Western suburban rolling stock underwent radical change; during the mid-1970s the prototype PEP sliding door trains appeared and saw regular use, but for series production the Class 508 units were adopted and arrived in August

Right:
'Merchant Navy' Pacific No 35005 *Canadian Pacific* **propels the 3.54pm Clapham Junction to Exmouth Junction empty milk tank train out of the Kensington sidings on to the Longhedge line prior to setting off via East Putney to the main line, on 25 June 1951.** *Brian Morrison*

1979. However, these were only a stop-gap and moved on to Merseyside when the SR's own design, the Class 455, was delivered in 1983, enabling the last of the veteran 4-SUB units to be withdrawn and the remaining 4-EPB (Class 415) units to be transferred to other divisions.

Since 1860 the main and Windsor lines out of Waterloo have formed separate routes. It is possible to cross from the up main to up Windsor and from the down Windsor to main lines just west of Queenstown Road, a connection primarily intended to give access to and from Nine Elms yard. Since May 1990, a ladder crossover has been provided in the opposite direction to the east of Queenstown Road station. Until the 1906-08 widenings, it was also possible to cross from the main to the Windsor and Ludgate lines (but not to the West London) east of Clapham Junction. The remaining links between the two sections are firstly, the circuitous route from Byfleet Junction via Chertsey to Virginia Water and, secondly, the line from Wimbledon to Point Pleasant Junction via East Putney. The junction at Wimbledon was remodelled in 1899 to improve through running.

This line was served principally by the frequent trains of the District Line as well as a LSWR steam service from Waterloo. MDR plans for quadrupling were abandoned in 1913 and the line soon saw the first LSWR electric trains, with public services starting on 25 October 1915. The initially frequent service was reduced in 1918 and never gained the patronage of most other Southern electric routes. After the outbreak of war in 1939, the service was confined to the peak hours and following disruption by enemy action during 1940 it was officially withdrawn from 5 May 1941. However, from the end of the war until 1962, there were a number of Saturday afternoon through trains (mostly from the Alton line) into Waterloo by this route. The line used to see much excursion and special traffic between the South Western main line and the West London Extension and Longhedge routes — an example of the latter were the regular pre-1939 excursions between Portsmouth and Sheerness. During the 1970s the SR occasionally ran 'Merrymaker' excursions to the seaside from Southfields, which otherwise was never served by Southern trains.

The SR has always resisted Underground attempts to take over the East Putney Line as it provides access to Wimbledon Park sidings for the stream of empty electric trains leaving Waterloo at the end of the morning rush hour. Conversely, the yard despatches empty trains towards Waterloo in the early morning and prior to the evening rush hour. The line was also used by milk and van trains from the main line bound for the Kensington sidings at Clapham Junction; a well known working was the 3.54pm empty milk tanks from Clapham Junction to Exmouth Junction, a substantial train which sometimes required

Below:
Even a 'Merchant Navy' could not always tackle the bank to East Putney with this heavy empty milk train; here pilot assistance is being provided by 'M7' tank 30130.
Lens of Sutton

Above:
East Putney station on 12 March 1981, with a 4-SUB unit on a down empty stock working to Wimbledon Park (headcode 03). The buildings on the island platform have since been demolished. *Ian Allan Library — J.G.Glover*

Below:
London Underground 'D78' stock forms an eastbound District line train at Wimbledon Park as a Class 455 unit approaches with an empty working to the sidings on 15 March 1989. The 1889 box on the platform remained in use until February 1991. *Author*

Above:
'West Country' 4-6-2 No 34007 *Wadebridge* brings a theatrical special from the LMR off the East Putney line at Wimbledon on to the down main line on 31 March 1957. No 34007 had been assisted by 34095 as far as East Putney.   *Author*

Right:
Having come from Clapham Junction via East Putney and crossed over to the Sutton line at Wimbledon 'B' box, the Morden milk tank train passes Wimbledon West yard hauled by No 4681, one of the WR pannier tanks then allocated to Nine Elms, on 8 July 1961. *Author*

Below right:
Adams 'O2' class 0-4-4T E233 shunting in Clapham Yard c1930. *Lens of Sutton*

double heading up the 1 in 60 gradient to East Putney.

The condition of the viaduct carrying the up line over the Windsor lines near East Putney began to cause concern in 1983 and it had to be closed to all traffic from 3 April 1987. Under the WARS scheme, the down line was to be resignalled for bi-directional working, so in the meantime the small number of up empty trains via East Putney was diverted via the main line. Through running between the up main and East Putney lines at Wimbledon was severed on 19 March 1989 and in the down direction from 15 April 1990, but it was still possible to work empty trains through Wimbledon Park sidings. The new Wimbledon signalling centre took over from Point Pleasant Junction box in September 1990, and from the other boxes at East Putney, Wimbledon Park and Wimbledon 'A' on 24 February 1991, thus restoring through working in both directions over the East Putney line, which had been sorely missed during the aftermath of the Clapham Junction disaster.

Little has been said so far about the long distance trains passing through Clapham Junction — the LSWR's salmon and brown coaches behind Adams or Drummond 4-4-0s, the SR's Maunsell corridor stock headed by a 'King Arthur' or 'Lord Nelson' 4-6-0 and finally the combination of Bulleid Pacifics and carriages in malachite green or one of the BR liveries. Almost invariably they passed through the station without stopping, although at the 40mph maximum permitted round the sharp curve followed by the main line tracks.

However, Clapham Junction played a key role in Waterloo's main line traffic as the principal carriage sidings were situated there from the 1860s. Originally, there was one group of sidings, with a carriage shed, placed between the Kensington and Windsor Line stations, while more sidings were laid out in the angle between the Windsor and main lines. The realignment of the Windsor lines in 1876 transferred the running lines to the north of the first group of sidings and these then adjoined the others. Nevertheless, as late as 1936, maps showed Clapham Yard as divided into the 'Yard Sidings', nearest to the Windsor Line, and the 'Park Sidings' adjacent to the main line. The origin of the latter name may have come from the extensive grounds which surrounded the large houses in St John's Hill during the 1860s, of which No 56 (used by the Signal Engineer) is the sole survivor.

The 1867 working timetable listed 15 trains formed at Falcon Sidings — among them the stock for the 10.50am Exeter express from Waterloo, which was to be brought up by the engine for the 11.10am to Southampton, while the stock for the 3.10pm to Southampton was to be hauled by the loco of the 3.15pm to Kingston with the train engine coupled at the rear (a predecessor of the 'top and tail' working sometimes seen with the Class 50s and the West of England stock during the 1980s). An accident investigation in 1899 recorded that every important main line train running into Waterloo was afterwards run back to Clapham Junction carriage sidings for remarshalling and cleaning — usually over 1,000 carriages were dealt with every day.

In the June 1913 working timetable, 31 empty trains left Clapham Yard for Waterloo on weekdays; this did include some outer suburban and semi-fast workings, but most local stock was berthed at Wimbledon Park, and sometimes on its way into Waterloo carried passengers from Earlsfield onwards. Empty trains returning to Clapham Yard followed the Windsor Line, usually entering the sidings at West London Junction. By the 1930s the yard occupied 10 acres, had 52 roads and could accommodate 640 vehicles. In 1927, £70,000 was spent on a new carriage shed, and a mechanical carriage washing machine was provided in 1934, spanning two of the reception roads at the West London Junction end of the yard. There was also a repair shop for the maintenance of rolling stock.

July 1939 saw 24 express and three semi-fast trains being formed at Clapham Yard on Mondays to Fridays. Many of the summer Saturday extras were stabled in suburban sidings, but it was the practice to bring them up to Clapham during the week for washing and cleaning. Besides these regular trains, the yard provided stock, including Pullman cars, for the many boat trains to and from Southampton Docks. Shunting in the yard was mainly done by Adams 'O2' 0-4-4Ts, with the help during the 1930s of the ex-KESR 0-8-0T *Hecate*. The empty trains to and from Waterloo were invariably hauled by 'M7' 0-4-4Ts, unless a train engine could be employed.

As late as 1958, work at Clapham Yard had hardly changed — every Bournemouth and West of England express (34 of them on a mid-week day) returned from Waterloo to be serviced and remarshalled. Bournemouth trains were the simpler ones to deal with — but the up 'Royal Wessex', which arrived formed in the order Weymouth-Swanage-Bournemouth West, for its return at 4.35pm required to be reassembled in the same sequence but in the opposite direction. The 'Atlantic Coast Express' was far more complicated with its winter 13-coach formation bound for Ilfracombe, Torrington, Padstow, Bude, Plymouth, Exeter Central, Exmouth, Sidmouth and Seaton. All these (mainly) brake corridor composites had to be formed into the correct order and labelled; except for the Exeter restaurant cars, none of the portions would return until the next day and then not all on the same train. The yard also had the task of assembling the overnight mail and newspaper trains: the 1.15am to the West of England was formed of 16 vehicles — five passenger coaches, each going to Ilfracombe, Bideford, Plymouth, Padstow and Yeovil, plus 11 vans for 10 destinations, including Weymouth and Bulford.

Right:
Ex-LBSCR 'E4' 0-6-2T No 32476 is busy marshalling stock for a West of England train on 25 July 1956; attached to the loco is a shunters' truck converted from an old Beattie tender. *Brian Morrison*

Below:
Diesel traction has just taken over shunting duties in the yard on 20 April 1958 when BR standard 350hp 0-6-0 No D3048 hauls out Pullman car *Hawthorn* and vans of LMS and LNER origin. *Author*

At this period the only important train not formed at Clapham Yard was the 'Bournemouth Belle', which between 1946 and 1960 was based at Stewarts Lane. It was worked round to Clapham Junction by whatever loco was available — anything from a 'C' class 0-6-0 to a 'Merchant Navy' Pacific complete with 'Golden Arrow' insignia. In fact, the 'Golden Arrow' itself was stabled at Clapham Yard prior to its demise in 1972. The yard was less busy on summer Saturdays than on normal weekdays; after the morning exodus of empty trains towards Waterloo, most Bournemouth line arrivals were turned round in the terminus to secure maximum use of rolling stock.

The 'O2' tanks had faded away during the 1940s and were replaced in the yard by a pair of ex-LBSCR 'E4' 0-6-2Ts, but in March 1958, BR 350hp diesel-electric shunters took over. During the early 1960s, Class 03 diesel-mechanical locos sometimes appeared, and later the Class 08s were succeeded by the SR's own 25mph Class 09 variety, as one of the Clapham duties involved taking milk tanks up the Windsor Line to Vauxhall and Waterloo. On the empty workings to and from Waterloo, the 'M7s' began to be replaced in 1959 by ex-GWR pannier tanks, then from 1963 these also gave way to BR Class 3 2-6-2Ts. One working during the 1950s was always performed by a Feltham 'H16' 4-6-2T, which was dia-

grammed for some of the heaviest tasks; the carriage working notices used to specify a tank engine to be used on some of the longest trains, as a tender (train) loco would take up too much room in Waterloo's relatively short platforms.

In 1967 12 sidings were electrified and the usual variety of SR EMUs could be seen in the yard. Loco-hauled stock was still based at Clapham for the first two Exeter departures and the Channel Islands boat trains. In 1978 there were still seven nightly mail and newspaper trains to be formed, including the 22.52 TPO train to Weymouth. The yard also acted as a staging point for mail and parcels traffic from Southampton, Brighton, Reading and Bricklayers Arms bound for such diverse destinations as Stranraer, Edinburgh and Liverpool Street.

With diminishing parcels traffic and the few loco-hauled trains composed of fixed formations, the need for diesel shunters at Clapham Yard ended. In 1987 the maintenance of the mail and parcels vans was transferred to Eastleigh, which also undertook the marshalling of the 22.52 Weymouth mail and of the newspaper trains. This arrangement was short-lived as the mail train lost its passenger section in May 1988 and was withdrawn completely in October. The occasional boat trains which are now run in connection with cruise liner sailings from Southampton

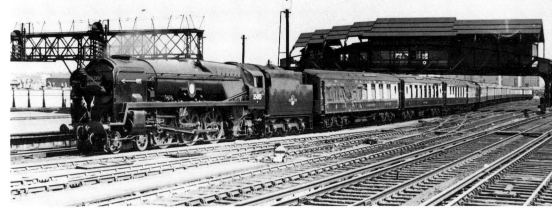

Docks are formed of a Mk 2 first class corridor set based at Eastleigh. The cessation of newspaper carriage on BR from 10 July 1988 caused the cancellation of three more trains, and Waterloo's night departures have since been reduced to one EMU to Southampton.

Clapham Junction was an important centre for milk traffic; in 1913, five up trains (all but one from the West Country) were booked to call at the loop platform to unload, and as many as 500 churns a day were transferred to the LBSCR for distribution to South London dairies. During the 1930s, churns were replaced by tank wagons and some of these were pumped off from the dock sidings into road vehicles above. Much of the milk traffic was now dealt with in the six Kensington sidings to the north of the Windsor Line. Here milk trains arriving via East Putney or Chertsey were split into sections for the distribution depots, such as Kensington Olympia, Vauxhall, Mottingham and Morden South, which in 1959 had three trips daily from Clapham Junction. After the Western Region had taken over beyond Salisbury, the West of England milk trains were transferred to the Berks & Hants line in 1964, and Clapham Junction lost some of its importance as WR diesels worked direct from Acton to Morden. One of Clapham's Class 09 diesels

Above:

A Battersea to Brent freight, mainly formed of empty coal wagons, passes beneath 'A' box behind LMR '3F' 0-6-0 No 43261 on 25 June 1951. *Brian Morrison*

took milk tanks each morning to Vauxhall, but this ceased in 1976 as rail haulage of milk traffic diminished.

Freight at Clapham Junction has usually involved trains passing through rather than stopping for loading or marshalling. In its early days some traffic from the main line to the north via Willesden was exchanged there, and as late as 1899 some LNWR freight trains via the West London line made Clapham Junction their nominal destination. Before Feltham Yard was constructed much of the LSWR's freight transfer traffic was marshalled in Nine Elms

yard, in addition to its London business originating there. In 1913 Clapham Junction saw 17 freight trains from Nine Elms to the main line and nine for the Windsor Line, as well as five GNR goods trains via the Widened Lines and Longhedge Junction bound for the small sorting sidings at Brentford.

Freight traffic in 1948 following the end of World War 2 was still heavy; Nine Elms now only handled SR business to the South of England, but had 10 main line and six Windsor Line departures. Cross-London transfers (predominantly of coal traffic) remained numerous with seven LMR or SR trains from Brent to Battersea via Kew, and eight ER workings from Ferme Park to Feltham via the Widened Lines. The SR also operated three transfer trips between Feltham and the South Eastern section via Longhedge and Factory Junctions.

By 1965, Nine Elms had only two main line departures, and the 1960s saw the ending of traffic at most

Left:
A Guildford via Cobham electric, fast to Surbiton, passes Clapham Cutting box during the late 1920s; the stock is one of the three-car units built in 1925 for this electrification.
LPC postcard — Author's collection

of the LSWR's suburban goods yards. Local freight activity finally ceased with the closure of Nine Elms yard in 1968 and Feltham marshalling yard in 1969.

The South Western Division's largest signalling centre was built in a corner of Feltham yard, taking control in 1974 of the Windsor Line west of Mortlake, the Hounslow Loop, the Kingston Roundabout and the Shepperton branch. Some of the manual boxes were retained to operate the numerous level crossings in the area until CCTV supervision was installed in 1976-77. A smaller panel box had been erected at Surbiton in 1970 (replacing the 1936 'glasshouse' style building) to control the station area and the lines towards Woking and Guildford as well as the Hampton Court branch. Local resignalling schemes also enabled colour lights to replace semaphores, and track circuit block working to eliminate intermediate

signalboxes. Raynes Park to Epsom was dealt with in 1966, the East Putney line in 1970 and the Chessington branch in 1972.

However, the main line out of Waterloo was still being operated by the signalling installed in 1936, much of it housed in LSWR boxes up to a century old. In contrast, the Central Division resignalling at Clapham Junction in 1980 replaced equipment dating only from 1952, while the neighbouring South Eastern panel took over from boxes built in 1959. Plan-

Below:
2-BIL unit No 2109 heads the 11.27 Waterloo to Portsmouth & Southsea through Clapham Cutting on 4 June 1966; the arches of Trinity Road bridge had not then been obscured by road widening. *Ian Allan Library — J.Scrace*

During the morning rush hour in 1964, commuters from Woking pack the corridors of 4-COR unit No 3115 while a train from Shepperton runs parallel on the up local line. The former 'D' or LSWR Main Line West box was situated in an alcove on the right hand side here.

Ian Allan Library — Brian Stephenson

Above:
The 10.06 Waterloo to Chessington train emerges from St John's Hill bridge on 5 December 1980, formed of unit 508.018.
Ian Allan Library — Brian Morrison

Right:
During the Class 33's reign on the Waterloo-Exeter service, No 6547 approaches Freemasons Bridge with the 15.00 train on 15 August 1973.
Ian Allan Library — Brian Morrison

ning for WARS began in 1978, but financial constraints adopted to obtain Department of Transport and Treasury approval limited its scope to replacement on a 'like for like' basis, without the major engineering works involved in earlier Southern Region projects. The choice of site for the new signalling centre was not easy; fortunately, in view of the subsequent Waterloo International station developments, it was decided to use some of the vacant land in Wimbledon West sidings.

The condition of the wiring in the 1936 box at Waterloo could not await the conclusion of discussions between BR and the DTp. On 5 February 1984, the three old power frames were replaced by a temporary panel; at the same time some track rationalisation was carried out between Waterloo and Vauxhall. Eventually, on 19 December 1984 ministerial approval was given for the £32.5 million WARS project. With failures of the life-expired equipment taking place, the first task was to instal small temporary panels in the old boxes at Raynes Park, New Malden and down the Epsom branch — this began with Raynes Park in February 1986 and concluded with New Malden two years later. Meanwhile, a building resembling a DIY warehouse was being erected at Wimbledon to house the new signalling centre. Plans drawn up in 1986 envisaged completion of the whole scheme during 1989.

Although no major alterations were planned, some of the old lattice girder signal gantries were replaced by lighter steel structures, and other signals were moved to obtain better sighting or spacing. It was wiring errors made during the commissioning of one of these re-positioned signals which brought about the disaster of 12 December 1988. This resulted in work on WARS being virtually halted, and plans for further temporary panel installations were abandoned — the existing panel at Waterloo was, however, moved to a temporary building in September 1990 to allow the 1936 box to be demolished.

Eventually, the Wimbledon signalling centre took over the main line in its immediate area (where track alterations had been made) during Easter 1990, followed by the Clapham Junction to Nine Elms section on 27 May 1990. Control from the new centre replaced the temporary panels at Raynes Park in May and those at New Malden, Motspur Park, Epsom and Leatherhead during July and August 1990. Operation of the East Putney line became its responsibility in February 1991, leaving only the Waterloo to Nine Elms area to be transferred to complete the WARS project. Following a four-day blockade during the Easter weekend, the Wimbledon centre took over the Waterloo area on 2 April 1991.

Below:
Electro-diesel No 73142 (not yet the royal engine) runs through Clapham Junction with a special West Country van train on 18 November 1974.
Ian Allan Library — Brian Morrison

South Western Lines Electric Headcodes

Electric Headcodes for Principal Services from Waterloo

	1939	1960	1990
Kingston Roundabout via Richmond	V (61)	61 (V)	(21)
Kingston Roundabout via Wimbledon	V (62)	62 (V)	(32)
Kingston only via Richmond		68 (d)	(68)
Hounslow Loop via Brentford	O (89)	89 (O)	(89)
Hounslow Loop via Richmond	O (87)	87 (O)	(89)
Guildford via Brentford & Chertsey			(99)
Shepperton via Kingston	S (24)	24 (S)	(24)
Shepperton via Richmond	S (47)	47 (S)	(47)
Strawberry Hill via Kingston	∧(63)	63 (∧)	(21)
Strawberry Hill via Richmond	∧(64)	64 (∧)	(32)
Wimbledon via East Putney	P (86)		
Wimbledon Park via East Putney	P		
Windsor via Brentford (splitting)	17 (H)	17 (H)	
Windsor via Brentford (through)	—	57 (T)	(57)
Windsor via Richmond (splitting)	18 (H)	18 (H)	
Windsor via Richmond (through)		58 (T)	(58)
Weybridge via Brentford	17	17	(13)
Weybridge via Richmond	18	18	(14)
Hampton Court	H (30)	30 (H)	(30)
Chessington South	L (18)	18 (L)	(18)
Epsom/(Leatherhead)	L (19)	19 (L)	(19)
Dorking/(Horsham)	I (17)	17 (I)	(17)
Effingham Jc via Epsom	I (15)	16 (I)	(16)
Guildford via Epsom	I (16)	16 (I)	(16)
Effingham Jc via Cobham	H (43)	42 (H)	(42)
Guildford via Cobham	H (42)	42 (H)	(42)
Woking	10 T	10 (T)	10
Chertsey via Weybridge	14 T	14 (T)	(14)
Woking via Brentford & Ascot	25 (I)	25	
Woking via Richmond & Ascot	26 (I)	26	
Reading via Brentford (fast)			37
Reading via Brentford (semi-fast)	27 (L)	27	39
Reading via Richmond (fast)			36
Reading via Richmond (semi-fast)	28 (L)	28	38
Aldershot via Brentford/Ascot (fast)			27
Aldershot via Brentford/Ascot (semi-fast)	37	37	29
Aldershot via Richmond/Ascot (fast)			26

Right:
2-EPB units Nos 5674 and 5676 form an up Hounslow Loop train, seen between Wandsworth Town and Clapham Junction on 19 November 1979. The far end of Clapham yard on the left extends nearly to Wandsworth Town station.
C.J.Marsden

	1939	1960	1990
Aldershot via Richmond/Ascot (semi-fast)	38	38	28
Ascot via Woking	20	20	
Guildford via Woking (slow)			75
Farnham (Surbiton stop)		52 (N)	
Farnham (No Surbiton stop)		72	
Farnham/Alton (splitting)	12	12 (O)	
Alton (through)		32 (N)	
Farnham/Alton (fast)			51
Farnham/Alton (semi-fast)			52
Farnham/Alton (slow)		—	53
Farnham via East Putney		53 (N)	
Alton via East Putney		02 (N)	
Portsmouth & Southsea (slow-splitting)	7	7 (d)	
Portsmouth & Southsea (slow-through)		57	
Portsmouth & Southsea (semi-fast — Havant stop)		70	
Portsmouth & Southsea (fast)			71
Portsmouth & Southsea (semi-fast)			72
Portsmouth & Southsea (slow)			73
Portsmouth & Southsea via Cobham			74
Portsmouth Harbour (fast)	8		81
Portsmouth Harbour (non-stop)		08	
Portsmouth Harbour (s/fast — no Havant stop)		8	
Portsmouth Harbour (s/fast — Havant stop)		80 (T)	82
Portsmouth Harbour (slow)		81	83
Portsmouth Harbour via Cobham			84
Portsmouth Harbour via East Putney		06	
Basingstoke/Salisbury/Exeter (fast)			61
Basingstoke/Salisbury/Exeter (semi-fast)			62
Basingstoke/Salisbury/Exeter (slow)			63
Weymouth Quay			90
Bournemouth/Poole/Weymouth (fast)			91
Bournemouth/Poole/Weymouth (semi-fast)			92
Bournemouth/Poole/Weymouth (slow)			93
Southampton Eastern Docks			95
Southampton Western Docks			96
Lymington Pier			97
Southampton via Havant			5
Eastleigh via Havant			7
Portsmouth & Southsea via Eastleigh			70
Portsmouth Harbour via Eastleigh			80

Miscellaneous Workings

Clapham Jc — Kensington Olympia			20

Empty trains to:

	1939	1960	1990
Clapham Yard via Down Main Line			00
Clapham Yard via Down Windsor Line			01
Clapham Yard via Up Main Loop			02
Wimbledon Park via East Putney		03	03
Wimbledon Park via Main Line			08
Clapham Yard — Stewarts Lane etc			55

Headcodes shown in brackets are alternatives not in regular use; thus in 1939 inner suburban services were worked by wooden-body units with letter headcodes, but by 1960 almost all of this pre-war stock had been replaced by SUB or EPB units with numerical headcodes. In 1990 South Western suburban services were monopolised by Class 455 units, which have no provision for headcodes, so the route numbers were largely theoretical.

The Passing Scene — Wednesday 6 July 1949

Time (pm)	Train	Loco	Class	Duty (SR)
2.32	Lillie Bridge-Peckham Rye freight	2554	C2X 0-6-0	
2.32	Milk tanks from Waterloo (Waterloo line)	S1544	H 0-4-4T	57
2.35	Light engine to Windsor line ex-Longhedge	69465	N1 0-6-2T	ER
2.38	Feltham-Clarence Yard freight	E9458	N1 0-6-2T	ER
2.39	2.30 Victoria-Tunbridge Wells	31745	D1 4-4-0	294
2.41	Empty stock to Waterloo (3.30)	30244	M7 0-4-4T	52
2.41	Norwood Jc-Willesden freight	48309	8F 2-8-0	LMR
2.41	Light Stewarts Lane to yard	31900	U1 2-6-0	
2.47	11.30 Weymouth-Waterloo	35028	MN 4-6-2	386
2.48	Empty stock to Waterloo (3.20)	319	M7 0-4-4T	
2.56	Vans from Waterloo to yard	676	M7 0-4-4T	59
2.57	2.50 Waterloo-Ilfracombe	34058	BB 4-6-2	7
3.02	2.54 Waterloo-Salisbury	30454	N15 4-6-0	432
3.02	Feltham-Hither Green freight	79203	8WD 2-8-0	
3.02	Empty stock from Waterloo (2.19)	667	M7 0-4-4T	50
3.08	Empty stock from Waterloo (2.27)	30132	M7 0-4-4T	51
3.10	Empty boat train, yard-Longhedge	31900	U1 2-6-0	
3.11	Light engine ex-Nine Elms (3.54 milk)	34051	BB 4-6-2	433
3.11	Norwood-Battersea freight	1912	W 2-6-4T	514
3.12	Battersea-Norwood freight	31918	W 2-6-4T	
3.20	Empty stock to Waterloo (3.54)	30241	M7 0-4-4T	60
3.21	Feltham-Nine Elms freight	483	H15 4-6-0	
3.26	3.20 Waterloo-Weymouth	35030	MN 4-6-2	382

Carriage marshalling was being done by M7 0-4-4T 33 (duty 65) and E4 0-6-2T 2500 (duty 63).

A down Chessington train, formed of a 4-SUB LBSCR type unit augmented by a steel trailer, approaches the station, while an up train headed by a 1925 design unit leaves for Waterloo. A 2-Nol unit of LSWR origin is passing on the Windsor Line, 8 November 1949.
Ian Allan Library — C.C.B.Herbert

3 The South Central Lines

In contrast to the variety of activity on the South Western lines, Clapham Junction has always played the lesser role of being mainly an important intermediate station on the Central lines. While the LSWR had two main radial routes out of Waterloo, the LBSCR had a complicated suburban system linking its original terminus at London Bridge with Victoria, long referred to in the timetables as its West End station. Concentric routes joined the two termini, and in addition there was a choice of circular services to and from London Bridge. Combined with the SECR's lines from Victoria, Holborn Viaduct and Blackfriars, South London was provided with a dense railway network which discouraged Underground penetration into the area. Nevertheless, during the 'Tube Mania' of the early 1900s, some optimistic promoters had proposed to build underground lines which would have linked Clapham Junction with Central London.

The pattern of routes established during the 19th century to convey white-collar workers from the inner suburbs to their daily tasks in the City began to be eroded when the clerks were enticed by the Southern Railway to move out into the new housing estates in Surrey and Kent. Since 1945 the inner suburbs have become the home of a cosmopolitan population employed in local industries and services which does not make much use of the railway, so that the network has fallen into progressive decline. This account of the train services on the Central side at Clapham Junction reflects the effect of these social changes on the railway.

When the West End of London & Crystal Palace Railway (WELCP) line was opened from Crystal Palace to Wandsworth Common on 1 December 1856, the existing service from London Bridge via Sydenham (started in June 1854) was extended to the new temporary terminus, providing 18 trains on weekdays and 10 on Sundays. When the WELCP was prolonged to Pimlico on 29 May 1858, the intermediate station at New Wandsworth was served by all 21 weekday trains to London Bridge as well as by seven of the nine trains from Pimlico to Croydon via Crystal Palace and Norwood Junction — a link opened in October 1857. Stations on the WELCP were provided

at Stewarts Lane (closed after a few months), New Wandsworth, Wandsworth Common, Balham Hill, Streatham (Hill was added to its name in 1869), Lower (now West) Norwood, Gipsy Hill and Crystal Palace.

The opening of the Victoria Station & Pimlico Railway (VS&P) on 1 October 1860 brought the closure of the original Pimlico terminus, but a Battersea station was provided nearby on the line into Victoria. By November 1861, New Wandsworth was being served by 21 trains to London Bridge and 19 locals to Croydon via Crystal Palace (on Sundays the figures were 11 and eight respectively). Passing through the station were also seven LBSCR fast trains to the coast and nine LCDR services (including four expresses) which were not allowed to stop between Victoria and Crystal Palace.

The direct route between Balham and Windmill Bridge Junction (outside Croydon) which opened on 1 December 1862, gave Victoria a main line equivalent to that from London Bridge. In May 1863, 14 longer distance trains left Victoria by this route, but suburban traffic to its stations at Streatham Common and Thornton Heath was slow to develop and only seven weekday stopping trains were provided. Stations were later added at Selhurst in May 1865 and at Norbury in January 1878. The newly opened station at Clapham Junction was served by seven of these fast main line trains as well as by 22 trains to London Bridge and 15 to Croydon via Crystal Palace (also three which did not stop).

The opening of the direct line to Croydon brought more traffic to the WELCP line, and a second up (local) track was added between the up main and the down lines from Balham Junction to Longhedge Junction. This involved resiting the station at Balham Hill, which was then renamed Balham, and altering the platforms at New Wandsworth. The LBSCR retained this station for six years after Clapham Junction had been built nearby, until the second station at Wandsworth Common opened on 1 November 1869.

The original WELCP/VS&P route via Stewarts Lane curved sharply under the LSWR main line and then climbed steeply to the Grosvenor Bridge over the Thames. After 1863 the line beyond Longhedge Junction was shared with the West London trains and at Stewarts Lane was joined by those of the LCDR coming from the Herne Hill direction. To provide a better approach to Victoria, a new high level cut-off line was opened on 1 December 1867. This departed from the original route at Pouparts Junction, named after the market gardens around Battersea owned by the well known firm of Covent Garden merchants. The three tracks rose on to a viaduct to cross over the WELCP route at Longhedge Junction, then the LSWR lines, meeting at York Road Junction the LBSCR's South London line, which had been opened on 1 May 1867. The original route was rejoined at Battersea Pier Junction, just south of the river. A station had been opened at York Road on 1 May 1867, which later took the name of Battersea Park after the earlier low level Battersea station closed in November 1870. Between there and Victoria, a station, which was primarily a ticket collecting platform, was opened on the river bridge at Grosvenor Road on 1 November 1870. The third road between Pouparts Junction and Longhedge Junction was converted into a refuge siding when the new line opened.

The South London line was part of the LBSCR's major expansion within the London area during the 1860s. Built in conjunction with the LCDR, it formed the innermost circle between Victoria and London Bridge via Clapham (now Clapham High Street), Denmark Hill and Peckham Rye. Fears of competitive exploitation by the LCDR, or others, of the rapidly-developing suburbs between the main lines from Victoria and London Bridge, led the LBSCR to build a new line, opened on 1 October 1868, from Peckham Rye to Sutton via Tulse Hill, Streatham, Mitcham Junction, Hackbridge and Carshalton. Connections were made with existing lines: from Tulse Hill to West Norwood Junction on 1 November 1870 and to Leigham Junction (towards Streatham Hill) on 1 August 1871, also from Streatham to Streatham Common on 1 January 1886.

A spur from Streatham North Junction on the Victoria-Croydon main line to Streatham South Junction

Below:
LBSCR 'D' tank No 33 *Mitcham* and 'B2' 4-4-0 No 315 *Duncannon* double head a down Portsmouth train near Wandsworth Common in the summer of 1899 — note the parallel arrangement of tracks.
Ian Allan Library — Bucknall collection

Right:
LBSCR 'B1' 0-4-2 193 *Fremantle* heads a long and varied train of non-bogie stock past Balham Intermediate box in 1898. *Ian Allan Library — L&GRP*

Below right:
'E5x' class 0-6-2T No 676 calls at Clapham Junction on the down through line with a train still formed of six-wheel stock, on 30 September 1921.
Ian Allan Library — H.C.Casserley

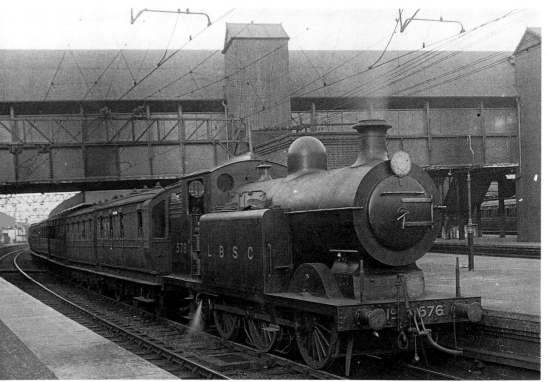

on the new line was provided on 1 October 1868, a day which also saw the opening of the LBSCR and LSWR joint line from there to Wimbledon. At Mitcham Junction (a new station), the Peckham Rye to Sutton line crossed the 1855 Wimbledon & Croydon Railway, but being the newcomer had to approach each of the junctions by a sharp curve. The new route, in conjunction with the opening in 1867 of the Horsham, Dorking & Leatherhead Railway, provided a direct line from both London Bridge and Victoria to the Mid-Sussex area. The original route to Sutton and Epsom had been the extension of the London & Croydon Railway from West Croydon opened on 10 May 1847. A branch opened from Sutton to Epsom Downs on 22 May 1865 brought the LBSCR within easy reach of the racecourse, and for many years this enjoyed Royal patronage.

The Brighton suburban network had now reached its full extent, and the new routes brought increased traffic to Clapham Junction. In August 1887, there were 83 suburban trains from Victoria on weekdays (almost all stopping at Clapham Junction) and 35 on Sundays — the LBSCR was a strict observer of the sabbath church interval and kept up the practice until the end of its existence. Besides the old-established Victoria-Crystal Palace-London Bridge circular route, 10 other services linked the two termini via Selhurst and Norwood Junction, while eight trains started from Clapham Junction to reach London Bridge via Streatham Hill and Tulse Hill. The new route to Sutton saw 17 trains on weekdays and six on Sundays. During the 1880s many of these trains would have been formed of Stroudley 'Terrier' tanks on sets of flimsy four-wheelers. The Crystal Palace service was augmented by five LNWR through trains from Willesden Junction to Croydon. Of the 23 weekday main line services from Victoria to Sussex and the coast, 18 called at Clapham Junction.

At the end of the 19th century the LBSCR was not noted for speed or punctuality, and with only one down road the Clapham Junction area was one of its bottlenecks. Therefore on 9 June 1895 a down local line from Pouparts Junction to Clapham Junction

North was added; after completion of the widening through the station already described, it was continued to Balham Junction in November 1895. At Wandsworth Common the station was rebuilt to accommodate the four tracks, but at Balham the new line ran at the back of the existing down platform, which was fenced off, and a new platform was built on the other side of the down local line, a peculiar arrangement which lasted until 1955. Quadruple track was extended beyond Balham in 1897 in the form of separate down and up lines for the Sutton direction, the down track rising on a flyover to join the London Bridge route at Streatham South Junction.

For the completion of quadrupling from the Streatham junctions to Windmill Bridge Junction, it was decided to adopt the alternate arrangement with a new pair of local lines being added on the down side. This involved the complete reconstruction of the stations between Streatham Common and Selhurst, where substantial new buildings were provided. The new layout was continued to Balham, and double-line spurs were built from the reinstated Streatham North Junction to the South Junction off both local and main lines. New signalboxes were provided at all three Streatham junctions and at Thornton Heath and Selhurst. All this work was carried out during the summer of 1903.

Quadrupling into Victoria was completed by a second up (main) line between Pouparts Junction and Battersea Park in 1905, crossing the Longhedge and LSWR lines on its own independent structure. (It was the 1867 bridges here which required renewal a century later.) The tracks between Battersea Park and Clapham Junction North were changed to the alternate arrangement in February 1907, and those beyond Clapham Junction to Balham in late 1908, so the completion of the station rebuilding saw from 13 March 1910 the new pairing with the local lines on the down side in use all the way from Victoria to Selhurst.

However, the LBSCR's inner suburban services, notably the South London line, began to suffer during the early 1900s from the competition of the electric tramcar, to which the rather infrequent trains, formed typically of a Billinton 0-6-2T and six-wheel stock, could not provide an adequate alternative. Services in August 1908 were little better than 20 years earlier, with 79 suburban trains leaving Victoria for Clapham Junction and nine more peak hour local trains not stopping there. In addition, there were 21 main line and 12 Mid-Sussex line trains calling, while nine residential fast trains during the late afternoon and evening were non-stop. However, most of the main line trains were designated in the timetable as stopping to pick up only, a prohibition which would have been strictly enforced at Victoria in days when its ticket barriers were manned by sharp-eyed collectors. The all-Pullman limited train to Brighton introduced in 1881 called at Clapham Junction each weekday

Above left:
A Crystal Palace to Victoria overhead electric train approaches Pouparts Junction, c1912. Signals on the Brighton's local lines can hardly be seen among the girders of the cantilever structures. To the right, the LSWR's pneumatic signals rise above the carriages standing in the reception sidings near West London Junction.
Courtesy of the National Railway Museum

Left:
As overhead ac traction nears its end, a train from Crystal Palace to Victoria, formed of a CP three-car unit, passes Wandsworth Common on 17 March 1928.
Ian Allan Library — H.C.Casserley

morning, until replaced by the 'Southern Belle' in November 1908. While suburban travellers were supposed to be in church, the Brighton ran some cheap Sunday excursions to the seaside for third-class passengers — one from Clapham Junction to Worthing at 9.05am preceded by a through train from Willesden Junction to Brighton.

The LBSCR decided to meet the threat from the tramcar by adopting electrification, using the 6,700 volts ac overhead system. The initial conversion of the South London line on 1 December 1909 did not affect Clapham Junction, but the next extension from Battersea Park to Crystal Palace brought electric trains to the area from 12 May 1911. From Pouparts Junction to Clapham Junction there was no room between the LBSCR and LSWR tracks to provide normal cross spans for the overhead wiring, so substantial cantilever structures were erected on the down side of the line to project the complicated ac catenary above the four tracks. After the ac electrification was abandoned in 1929, one of these gantries at Pouparts

Junction was used to carry semaphore signals, then in 1952 adapted for colour lights (in the opposite direction), but unfortunately it did not meet the requirements of the 1980 resignalling.

In 1912, electric traction was extended from Crystal Palace to Norwood Junction and to a maintenance depot at Selhurst. The line from London Bridge to Crystal Palace via Tulse Hill was also electrified during 1912, and an infrequent circular service was introduced from Victoria to London Bridge via Clapham Junction, Streatham Hill and Tulse Hill. A few of these trains actually started from Clapham

Below:
Police and Guardsmen protect loyal staff manning Pouparts Junction signalbox during the August 1911 railway strike. The South of England did not, however, experience the disruption and violence which accompanied this strike in other parts of the country.
Courtesy of the National Railway Museum (382/68)

Above:

A cantilever gantry built for the former overhead electrification carries Pouparts Junction up home signals, 17 May 1949. From October 1952 this gantry supported down line colour lights. West London Junction and Pouparts Junction boxes are just visible in the background. *British Rail*

Left:

Clapham Junction 'C' box starting signals and New Wandsworth distant signals stand at the country end of No 13 down through platform, on December 1949. The surrounding gloom is a reminder of the frequent need for the fog signalman's hut to be manned and the detonator placer brought into action. *R.F.Roberts*

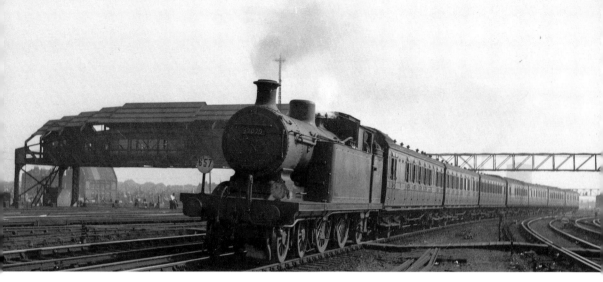

Above:
Marsh 'I3' 4-4-2T No 32029 approaches Clapham Junction with the 9.08am Victoria to Tunbridge Wells train in July 1949. *R.F.Roberts*

Junction and would have used the reversing siding at Pig Hill. Electric trains from Victoria to Crystal Palace ran four times per hour off-peak with some rush hour extras, but timings and intermediate stops were irregular.

The success of this electrification made the LBSCR decide in 1913 to convert the rest of its suburban network. In the Epsom direction, electric working would have terminated in a spacious station at Cheam, the line from Sutton having already been widened to four tracks. Coulsdon North would have been the limit of electrification on the main line. The electric traction equipment would again have been supplied by the German firm AEG, so the outbreak of war in 1914 soon brought work to a standstill. Subsequently, post-war economic conditions prevented any resumption of either the original, or the more ambitious main line schemes, which the Brighton was considering. The company was limited to a modest extension of elec-

trification from Balham via Selhurst to Wallington and Coulsdon North, on which some work had been done before the war.

It fell to the Southern Railway to complete this scheme on 1 April 1925, including its continuation into Sutton, where widening of the junction had to be carried out. The Sutton and Coulsdon lines were worked on Sir Herbert Walker's 20-minute interval principle; a few additional peak hour fast trains to Coulsdon did not stop at Clapham Junction and probably served to polish the wiring on the through lines.

The SR's decision to phase out ac traction in favour of third rail dc began with the conversion of the ser-

Right:
Ex-SECR locos also appeared on Oxted line trains: here D1 4-4-0 No 31509 calls at Clapham Junction with a train to Tunbridge Wells on 1 March 1950. *R. K. Kirkland*

vices from London Bridge to Crystal Palace and Streatham Hill on 17 June 1928, followed by the Victoria to Crystal Palace trains on 3 March 1929. The Victoria to Coulsdon and Sutton lines were gradually turned over to dc during the summer of 1929, the last ac trains running on 22 September. No longer would Clapham Cutting witness the banging and flashing which marked the passage of an overhead electric.

This conversion from ac was accompanied by further electrification of previously steam-operated routes: the third rail came into use below the ac catenary from Streatham Common to Selhurst and Sutton on 17 June 1928, when electric trains also began to run from London Bridge via Tulse Hill and Streatham to Sutton and Epsom Downs. On 3 March 1929, electric traction took over the service from Victoria to Mitcham Junction, Sutton and Epsom, where it joined the existing 1925 electrification from Waterloo in the new station at the junction. Central Section suburban services through Clapham Junction were now all-electric. A few pockets of steam still remained, however, including the single track Wimbledon to West Croydon line, converted on 6 July 1930.

The pattern of services provided trains every 20 minutes from Victoria and Clapham Junction to Beckenham Junction and to West Croydon via Crystal Palace, to Coulsdon North and to Epsom Downs via Selhurst, and to Epsom via Mitcham Junction. During the rush hours there were trains from Victoria to London Bridge via Streatham Hill and Tulse Hill, and extra fast trains to Coulsdon North, which were the only suburban services not stopping at Clapham Junction. No new vehicles had been provided for the Central Section suburban electrification; trains were made up of a mixture of conversions from LBSCR ac stock and from former steam-hauled coaches built by all three pre-Grouping companies.

In 1922, prior to grouping, of 44 main line departures from Victoria on weekdays, 26 picked up passengers at Clapham Junction — the exceptions included the 'Southern Belle' and the twice daily Newhaven Continentals. Under the SR this had been considerably reduced by 1931 to five trains for Brighton, one for Mid-Sussex and 10 for the Oxted line. Main line electrification to Brighton in 1933, to Eastbourne in 1935 and of the Mid-Sussex line in 1938 reduced Clapham Junction's role still further. It was served only by the hourly semi-fast and slow trains from Victoria to Brighton, also by a handful of Oxted steam trains — otherwise it was necessary to change at East Croydon or Sutton for the coast.

World War 2 and the restrictions on travel to the south coast drastically reduced Central Section main line services, with little more than the semi-fast and slow trains to Brighton remaining outside the morning and evening commuter periods. Off-peak suburban services were cut back to hourly frequency, Crystal Palace to Beckenham Junction became a shuttle, and London Bridge to Streatham Hill was withdrawn outside the rush hours. Recovery after the war was slow and after a decade the restored frequencies were reduced again at the end of the 1950s. However, Sundays and Bank Holidays during these years saw large crowds travelling at cheap fares filling every train to the seaside — many of these called at Clapham Junction and some started there, often formed of vintage suburban electric stock as the usual main line 6-PAN, 6-PUL and 4-COR units were quite insufficient for the weekend excursion traffic.

Below:
A semi-fast service to Brighton via Uckfield used to leave Victoria around 4pm. Here 'U1' class 2-6-0 No 31909 approaches Wandsworth Common with the 3.38pm train on 31 August 1957. *Author*

In contrast to the South Western, there were no berthing facilities at or near Clapham Junction to serve Victoria, in the manner that London Bridge was well provided with extensive sidings at New Cross Gate. The main electric depot at Selhurst was supplemented by sidings at Streatham Hill (part of the Brighton's 1913 electrification scheme) which were enlarged in 1938. Otherwise, there were a few sidings outside Victoria and at the various suburban terminals. The LBSCR had to go out to Streatham in 1905 to find a site for its carriage sidings; Eardley yard alongside Streatham South Junction had the merit of being equally accessible to Victoria and London Bridge. Following the electrification of most of the SR's Central Section, the yard was used to house spare Eastern Section stock for relief boat trains or Kent Coast weekend extras. For example, on a June Sunday in 1955, 11 empty trains were programmed to

Below:
The Brighton tanks were replaced by LMS design 2-6-4Ts around 1951. No 42089 passes Clapham Junction with the 2.08pm Victoria-Tunbridge Wells on 8 October 1955 — through rolling stock is still of pre-Grouping SECR origin. *Author*

Bottom:
Another LMS import was the '2MT' 2-6-2Ts, and one of these, No 41291, is in charge of a an empty boat train from Victoria to Eardley sidings, near Wandsworth Common, on 31 August 1957. *Author*

Right:
The Newhaven boat trains enjoyed a variety of motive power in the postwar years. Here the 9.05am relief service from Victoria is in the charge of 'King Arthur' No 30795 *Sir Dinadan*, approaching Clapham Junction in July 1949. *R.F.Roberts*

leave Eardley for Victoria — three to form Newhaven boat trains, and eight for Dover and Folkestone services. Some of these were to run via Tulse Hill and Herne Hill, others via Balham and Clapham Junction. After steam traction in Kent ceased during 1959-61, the yard fell into disuse (it had not been electrified) and was selected in the 1960s as the site of a motorway junction, which happily has not materialised, leaving nature to create a large area of woodland.

Hastened by the serious collision at Battersea Park on 2 April 1937, colour light signalling was installed between Pouparts Junction and Battersea Pier Junction on 16 October 1938 and was extended into Victoria Central Section on 4 June 1939. Interrupted by the outbreak of war, the Southern Railway in 1946 announced its intention to continue installing colour light signalling on the rest of the main lines from Victoria and London Bridge to Coulsdon, where it would link with the existing signals on the line to Brighton.

Already colour lights had replaced intermediate boxes at Streatham Common South and Norbury in 1936.

The remaining manual boxes at Pouparts Junction, Clapham Junction 'B' and 'C', New Wandsworth, Wandsworth Common, Balham Junction, Streatham North and South Junctions and Streatham Common were to be abolished, and control shared between new miniature lever power boxes at Clapham Junction (103 levers), Balham (43) and Streatham Junction (79). Postwar shortages delayed completion of this

Below:
On 8 May 1960, engineering work on the South Eastern side of Victoria diverted the 'Golden Arrow' to depart from the Central section via Crystal Palace and Beckenham Junction — this is No 34086 *219 Squadron* passing slowly through Clapham Junction on the down local line. *Author*

An annual event is the royal train to Tattenham Corner on Derby Day — on 6 June 1953, during Coronation week, the all-Pullman special passes Clapham Junction behind 'Schools' No 30915 *Brighton.* *Author*

On 13 April 1958, Atlantic No 32424 *Beachy Head* **made its last run on the RCTS 'Sussex Coast Limited' rail tour. At New Wandsworth the special is running neck and neck with the regular 10.25am to Littlehampton.** *Lens of Sutton*

work until October 1952: on the 5th, some 500 S&T staff were mobilised to convert the Streatham area, and the line was clear in plenty of time for the passage at 10.30am of *Beachy Head* on the RCTS Brighton Works Centenary special. The Clapham Junction to Balham section was dealt with the following Sunday, while the secondary suburban lines and branches retained semaphore signalling for a few more years. 1963 saw the first extension of colour lights from Streatham Junction to Mitcham Junction, but the major conversions took place in 1969 when a small panel in Streatham box took over the Streatham Hill to Tulse Hill area, linking at Gipsy Hill with an extension of Norwood Junction's control to Crystal Palace. In October 1969, semaphore signalling was replaced between Mitcham Junction and Sutton.

The 1952 resignalling had been based on prewar technology, but by the 1970s the SR had adopted the policy of centralised signal centres controlling wide areas by means of operating panels and closed-circuit television. The Clapham Junction centre covers the Central Division out to Cheam, West Croydon, Norbury and Crystal Palace, while its South Eastern panel controls the former LCDR lines as far as Otford and Longfield. The centre replaced 35 old boxes and supervises 267 miles of track; it took over the immediate area around Clapham Junction on 28 November 1980, Victoria Central side from 9 May 1981, then Balham on 7 June, Streatham Junction in two stages on 28 June and 9 August, West Croydon 'B' on 18 October, and finally Sutton on 4 October 1982.

Some track rationalisation was included in the scheme: Pouparts Junction was reduced to a single lead connection into the fast lines, and also singled was the fast line side spur between Streatham North and South Junctions. The original LCDR route from

Beckenham Junction to Bromley Junction, Crystal Palace was likewise singled. In earlier years it had been used as a diversionary route for South Eastern Division trains to and from Victoria, but the adaptation of the South London line (now the Atlantic line) for South Eastern use provided a better alternative. However, the works involved in the Channel Tunnel connection to Waterloo have required diverted trains to run via Crystal Palace and Clapham Junction again during 1990-91. The most drastic rationalisation affected the Epsom Downs branch which was singled in 1982 and subsequently curtailed to one simple platform in February 1989 — a contrast to the nine which the LBSCR needed to handle Derby Day traffic.

For the Derby, Her Majesty the Queen still travels from Victoria, but since Grouping, Epsom Downs has been replaced by the more conveniently situated SECR station at Tattenham Corner as the destination of the royal train, now customarily hauled by electro-diesel loco No 73201 *Broadlands*. It is also the custom to receive State visitors to Britain at Gatwick Airport and convey them by special train to their Royal welcome on platform 2 at Victoria, but as this is on the South Eastern side of the terminus, the specials usually travel via Tulse Hill and Herne Hill instead of the Central lines through Clapham Junction.

The decline of inner suburban traffic and the adoption of the five-day week has had its worst effects on the lines to London Bridge and to the other City termini. Many stations close early in the evening and at weekends — on Sundays, the once busy line from London Bridge to Tulse Hill sees no trains at all, and outside the peak hours there are no services between Streatham and Mitcham Junction. The circular routes have all but disappeared; Tulse Hill to Streatham Hill sees only a token service, provided by what would

otherwise be empty stock workings, to maintain the memory of the former London Bridge to Victoria service. London Bridge to London Bridge via Tulse Hill, Crystal Palace and Sydenham is confined to a few peak hour trains, while the outer circuit via Selhurst and Norwood Junction was severed in 1982 in connection with the remodelling of the Croydon area as part of the Three Bridges signalling scheme. This also led to the closure of Coulsdon North station (latterly used only in the rush hours) in October 1983, with the diversion of its trains to Smitham and the provision of a new service to Tattenham Corner from Victoria, a route hitherto worked only on prewar Sundays. The Tattenham Corner and the neighbouring Epsom Downs branches serve an area of low-density up-market housing with high car ownership and off-peak traffic now justifies only an hourly service — both upward and downward movements in economic factors can harm the railway!

Sliding door Class 455 stock began to be allocated to the Central lines in 1985, but not in sufficient quantity to operate the complete service, so that many refurbished Class 415 and 416 units (EPB stock) continued in use throughout the day. With the introduction of the Thameslink Class 319 stock in 1988, some of these units began to be seen regularly at Clapham Junction; the arrival of the second batch of Class 319s and the construction of the Class 456 two-car units in 1991 is intended to complete the replacement of the EPB slam-door stock.

On the main line, the first generation electric stock, the 6-PUL, 6-PAN, 4-COR and 4-LAV units, were replaced during the 1960s by four-car sets — CIGs and BIGs (Classes 421 and 422) for the fast services, VEPs (Class 423) for the semi-fasts. Today's electric multiple-units undoubtedly lack the glamour of the steam 'Southern Belle' with its Baltic tank, or 'King Arthur' 4-6-0, succeeded in 1933 by the electric Pullman which assumed the title of 'Brighton Belle' in 1934 — old age led to its much-regretted withdrawal in 1972. Another prestigious service in the past was the Newhaven Continental, long associated with the Brighton Atlantics and a regular working during the 1950s of the SR's three original electric locos. In 1970 it ceased to be loco-hauled and today it is just another EMU, sometimes merely detached from a Brighton semi-fast at Haywards Heath. When running as an independent train, until recent years it followed

On 14 May 1984, the inaugural day of the 'Gatwick Express' push and pull service, an up train headed by GLV 9106 passes New Wandsworth. A Dorking to Victoria train is being overtaken on the local line, while the short-lived New Wandsworth crossover is visible between the two trains. *C.J.Marsden*

Above:
During the 1988/89 timetable, Class 319 units had a regular semi-fast working to Victoria on the 15.28 from Hassocks; No 319.056 is seen passing New Wandsworth on 13 April 1989. The '319' units have since become increasingly familiar on South Central suburban services. *C.J.Marsden*

the 1860 low level route from Pouparts Junction via Stewarts Lane into Victoria South Eastern side, where Continental traffic has been concentrated.

If maritime traffic has declined, air travel through Gatwick Airport has been the growth area. The original 1936 aerodrome was linked to Clapham Junction every hour by the Brighton semi-fast trains. When the station for the new airport was opened in 1958, a two-car unit (usually a 2-HAL) was attached there to the half-hourly Horsham to Victoria service. Soon these were supplemented by extra trains to and from Gatwick only, and by an all-night service. During the 1970s the four-times-per-hour service to the airport was marketed as the 'Rapid City Link' and equipped with VEP units modified to give extra space for baggage, coded 4-VEG. Finally in 1984 the 'Gatwick Express' service was launched providing a 15-minute service of non-stop push and pull trains worked by Class 73 locos attached to sets of Mk 2 air-conditioned stock. Under sectorisation this has become an InterCity operation within Network SouthEast territory.

In May 1978 the growing traffic from Gatwick Airport and from Croydon's commercial activity prompted a radical revision of Central Division services. Mid-Sussex line trains were diverted from the Sutton and Dorking route to run via Three Bridges and call at Gatwick, which was also served by the Hastings and Littlehampton trains and the Brighton semi-fasts, and from May 1988 by the Thameslink through workings to Bedford. All off-peak trains now call at East Croydon — the hourly fast trains from Victoria to Brighton make the extra stop within their existing non-stop timing.

Restoration of main line services to Clapham Junction began in May 1978 with the Mid-Sussex trains, followed in May 1984 by those to Littlehampton and Hastings and from October 1987 by the new electric trains to the Oxted line, which had been the last stronghold of steam on the Central Division, diesel traction taking over the Victoria services in 1962. Diversion of the Mid-Sussex trains caused great discontent among Dorking residents, and from May 1987 they were placated by an hourly Victoria to Horsham semi-fast service, running non-stop to Sutton — an exception to the rule that all suburban-type trains call at Clapham Junction as old EPB stock was normally employed.

As an alternative to the LSWR's East Putney line, a second means of connecting the Central and South Western sections is provided by the link from Streatham to Wimbledon. Built jointly by the LBSCR and the LSWR and opened on 1 October 1868, this line left the LBSCR at Streatham South Junction and split at Tooting Junction into two branches — one via Merton Abbey joined the West Croydon to Wimbledon line at Merton Park, while the other ran direct to Wimbledon with a station at Haydons Lane (now Road). LSWR trains from Ludgate Hill to Wimbledon usually took the clockwise route around this loop,

Above:
The Streatham to Wimbledon line provides a second link between Central and South West lines. Bridge renewal during 1957 diverted the Stewarts Lane to Clapham Junction 'Bournemouth Belle' empty stock via Herne Hill, Tulse Hill and Wimbledon, where on 12 May it is seen arriving behind 'C' class 0-6-0 No 31575 and 'N' class 2-6-0 No 31412.
Author

Below:
Occasionally the Streatham to Wimbledon route was used in the opposite direction to relieve Waterloo at times of pressure. On 13 March 1960 a train from Southampton Docks, headed by No 34094 *Mortehoe*, passes Wimbledon 'B' junction on its way to Victoria. *Author*

while LBSCR trains from London Bridge ran anti-clockwise. World War 1 led to the withdrawal of passenger services from 1 January 1917 and the two companies were reluctant to restore them after the war until the threat of the City & South London tube extension to Morden compelled their resumption from 27 August 1923.

The Southern Railway also promised to electrify the line, and this was carried out between Streatham South Junction and Wimbledon via Haydons Road on 3 March 1929, but the Tooting Junction to Merton Park branch was then closed to passenger traffic. As the new Wimbledon & Sutton railway was completed in stages, electric trains were extended over it and from 5 January 1930 began to operate a 'figure of eight' service from Holborn Viaduct via Tulse Hill, Wimbledon, Sutton, West Croydon and Crystal Palace to Victoria.

The subsequent history of this service illustrates the many changes introduced to match the declining traffic within the inner suburban area. At the City end, when weekend traffic from Holborn Viaduct and Blackfriars ceased to be viable, for a few months in 1977/78 trains were diverted from Streatham South Junction into Victoria, thus offering a Central Division alternative route from Clapham Junction to Wimbledon. In the 1978 timetable revision, the off-peak City terminal became London Bridge, but a few peak-hour trains still ran to Holborn Viaduct; from May 1988 these were extended via Thameslink to St Albans or Luton. South of Streatham Junction these followed a circular route via Wimbledon, Sutton and Mitcham Junction — clockwise in the morning, anti-clockwise in the evening. For several years this loop formed part of the off-peak London Bridge-Wimbledon-London Bridge circuit on Mondays to Fridays, but at weekends trains returned from Sutton to London Bridge via West Croydon and Forest Hill. By 1986 all weekday off-peak services followed this route while Sunday services had ceased on the Central lines at Wimbledon. The most recent change has been the restoration of the 'figure of eight' pattern with the service operating from London Bridge to Victoria via Wimbledon, Sutton, West Croydon and Selhurst.

The Central and South Western lines were linked in the down direction by a crossover at the east end of Wimbledon station. From June 1939 this was used regularly by the 'Flying Boat Specials' from Victoria to Southampton. The up trains had to run via East Putney and Longhedge Junction until an up line con-

Left:
Engineering work, probably in the Sutton area, had diverted the 11.02 Victoria to Bognor via Wimbledon on 23 February 1969: 4-CEP units Nos 7169 and 7115 are crossing over to the South Western line opposite 'A' box. *Author*

nection was provided (at government expense) in the
autumn of 1941 alongside Wimbledon 'C' box. These
links have also provided a useful diversionary route
for Mid-Sussex line trains when engineering works
have been taking place in the Sutton area.

These original connections at Wimbledon were
replaced as part of the Victoria resignalling scheme
by two sets of ladder crossovers providing interchange in both directions between the South Western
and Central lines, referred to as Wimbledon West
Junction. The Clapham Junction signalling centre
took over from the LSWR 'B' box (at the junction of
the West Croydon line) on 23 May 1982 and from the
SR-built 'C' box (at the divergence of the Sutton line)
on 1 August 1982.

The connections were used for stock movements
between Selhurst and East Wimbledon depots and by
a daily trip from Richmond to Selhurst by a Class 416
(2-EPB) unit off the North London line until Class
313 units replaced them. Coal trains off the West
London line, originating at Willesden, Acton or Didcot, latterly used this route from Clapham Junction to

reach Wimbledon West Yard or the concentration
depots on the Chessington branch in preference to
the busy and steeply-graded East Putney line. Coal
traffic to these depots has now ceased, but aggregate
trains still run occasionally to Tolworth yard. However, the most important train to traverse Wimbledon
West Junction was the VSOE Pullman which operated a Saturday 'Bournemouth Belle' service from
Victoria during the 1988 and 1989 seasons. In common with the junction off the East Putney line, this
connection was taken out of use from Easter 1990,
but problems with the interface between the new
Wimbledon signalling centre and the Central panels
at the Clapham Junction centre have caused an indef-
inite delay in its restoration.

Below:
**The Croydon to Wood Lane milk tanks seen near
Wandsworth Common on 31 August 1957 with 'C' class
0-6-0 No 31578.** *Author*

In contrast to its passenger operations, freight was
not a major part of the LBSCR's business. It dealt
with its West End freight traffic at Battersea Wharf
yard, which for many years was also used for sorting
'foreign' traffic. Of 18 departures in 1922, nine were
transfer trips to Norwood Junction marshalling yard;
main line freights ran to Brighton, Eastbourne, Horsham, Crawley and Three Bridges. These trains used
the original low level lines via Longhedge Junction
and joined the main line from Victoria at Pouparts
Junction. In addition to the LBSCR's own trains, a
similar number of freight workings came off the West
London line at Clapham Junction — four from Willesden Junction to Norwood, five from Old Oak Common to Norwood and two to Three Bridges. The GWR
worked one goods to Norwood from Park Royal, and
it had a milk train to East Croydon.

The pattern had changed little 30 years later; Battersea yard then despatched four main line goods,
nine transfer trips to Norwood and two local workings — to East Croydon via Crystal Palace and to
Eardley sidings calling en route at New Wandsworth
and Wandsworth Common. From the West London
there were eight Willesden to Norwood transfers (five
of them worked by the LMR, probably with ex-LNWR
7F 0-8-0s or Stanier 8F 2-8-0s) and four trains from
Old Oak Common to Norwood. In addition there was
a local goods from Lillie Bridge to Peckham Rye. The
LBSCR goods yard serving the Clapham Junction area
was that at New Wandsworth — the 1956 RCH list
indicated that it handled general goods, coal, live-
stock and furniture. As part of the wholesale reduction in local goods depots it closed on 7 October
1968. The site is now occupied by a housing estate.

A Battersea to Norwood Junction transfer freight passes
Clapham Junction on 26 June 1951 behind 'W' class 2-6-4T
No 31917. *Brian Morrison*

Central Lines Electric Headcodes

Headcodes for Principal Services from Victoria

	AC	1939	1960	1990
Streatham Hill	2			
London Bridge via Tulse Hill	5	H(Down)	01 (H)	
London Bridge via Tulse Hill	5	H (Up)	01 (H)	
Crystal Palace	1			
Beckenham Jc via Crystal Palace		P	36 (P)	86
Norwood Jc via Crystal Palace	3			
West Croydon via Crystal Palace	8	P̄ (06)	06 (P)	94
East Croydon via Crystal Palace	12	(L)	41 (L)	76
Coulsdon North via Crystal Palace		12 L	41 (L)	
Norwood Jc via Streatham Common		H̲	82 (H̲)	
Selhurst via Streatham Common	7	S	32 (S̲)	02
East Croydon via Streatham Common			08 (I)	72
Coulsdon North via Streatham Common	11	I̲	94 (I̲)	
Smitham/Tattenham Corner (slow)		I	38 (I)	72
Smitham/Tattenham Corner (fast)				74
Caterham via Streatham Common		Ī	80 (L)	
Sanderstead via Streatham Common				82
West Croydon via Streatham Common		S̄	30 (S)	92
Sutton/Epsom via Streatham Common	9	S	30 (S)	90
West Sutton via Streatham Common				68
Epsom Downs via Streatham Common		S	84 (S)	92
Epsom Downs via Mitcham Jc		O	0 (O)	96
Dorking/Horsham via Mitcham Jc		∧	86 (∧)	84
Epsom/(Effingham Jc/Guildford)		V	02 (V)	84
East Grinstead				66
Uckfield				88
Reigate via Redhill		34	34	10
Gatwick Airport via Quarry				20
Gatwick Airport via Redhill				30
Newhaven Harbour via Quarry			76	52
Seaford via Quarry		68	68	52
Eastbourne via Quarry		62	62	50
Eastbourne via Redhill		64	64	60

Right:
During the 1970s, block trains from Acton served Purley, Tolworth and Chessington coal concentration depots several times a day. Class 73 electro-diesel No E6040 has attached two diesel brake tenders to control its train of unfitted wagons, seen passing Wandsworth Common on 9 May 1972.
Ian Allan Library — J.Scrace

	AC	1939	1960	1990
Ore via Quarry/Eastbourne		52	52	50
Ore via Redhill/Eastbourne		72	72	60
Ore via Quarry/Direct		54	54	
Brighton via Quarry (fast)		4	4	4
Brighton via Quarry (semi-fast)		6	6	14
Brighton via Redhill (semi-fast)		12	12	34
Brighton via Redhill (slow)		14	14	44
Littlehampton via Quarry and Hove		16	16	2
Littlehampton via Redhill and Hove		18	18	12
Littlehampton via Mitcham Jc		50	50	
Littlehampton via Redhill/Horsham		58	58	32
Bognor Regis via Mitcham Jc		40	40	(84)
Bognor Regis via Quarry/Horsham		46	46 (L)	6
Bognor Regis via Redhill/Horsham		48	48 (T)	16
Bognor Regis via Quarry/Horsham/Littlehampton		96	96	22
Bognor Regis via Redhill Horsham/Littlehampton		98	98 (Down)	32
Bognor Regis via Redhill/Horsham/Littlehampton		98	42 (Up)	32
Bognor Regis via Redhill and Hove				40
Portsmouth Harbour via Mitcham Jc		20	20	
Portsmouth Harbour via Quarry/Horsham		26	26	8
Portsmouth Harbour via Redhill/Horsham		28	28	18
Portsmouth Harbour via Quarry and Hove				38
Southampton via Quarry and Hove				46
Southampton via Redhill and Horsham				36

Miscellaneous Workings
Empty trains to:

	AC	1939	1960	1990
Streatham Hill			01	08
Selhurst			32	02

Headcodes for 1939 are based on the general use of wooden-body stock with letter codes. By 1960 most inner suburban services were worked by SUB and EPB units with numerical codes. However, prewar stock still appeared on weekend excursions and relief trains to the coast, usually carrying numerical headcodes; sometimes letter codes were used, but no list of these was included in the working timetables. Although most Central suburban services from Victoria in 1990 were worked by Class 455 stock, numerical headcodes could be seen on EPB and Class 319 units.

The Passing Scene — Saturday 1 August 1959

Time (pm)	Time Due	Reporting Number	Train	Loco	Class	Duty (SR)
12.08	12.03	250	Empty stock to Waterloo (12.30)	30516	H16 4-6-2T	
12.09			Battersea-Brent freight	48339	8F 2-8-0	LMR
12.10	12.12	251	6.37 Exeter C.-Waterloo	35026	MN 4-6-2	524
12.14	12.14s		12.08 Victoria-Tunbridge Wells	80019	4MT 2-6-4T	
12.18	12.19	252	10.00 Bournemouth C.-Waterloo	30864	LN 4-6-0	
12.27	12.27s		10.47 Tunbridge Wells-Victoria	80153	4MT 2-6-4T	
12.27	12.25	253	8.25 Weymouth-Waterloo	35002	MN 4-6-2	
12.29	12.29	255	8.30 Exeter C.-Waterloo	73118	5MT 4-6-0	18
12.30	12.29	448	12.22 Waterloo-Bournemouth W.	30851	LN 4-6-0	251
12.33 arr) WL			Relief Hastings to Coventry	31411	N 2-6-0	
12.41 dep)			via Luton and Bedford	760xx	4MT 2-6-0	LMR
12.38	12.37	449	12.30 Down Bournemouth Belle	35014	MN 4-6-2	33
12.44	12.42	450	12.35 Waterloo-Weymouth	34095	WC 4-6-2	37
12.47	12.32	256	9.15 Swanage-Waterloo	34039	WC 4-6-2	386
12.49			Empty stock ex Waterloo (Boat)	30520	H16 4-6-2T	146
12.50	12.49	451	12.42 Waterloo-Basingstoke	31786	L1 4-4-0	11

Time (pm)	Time Due	Reporting Number	Train	Loco	Class	Duty (SR)
12.52	12.37	257	10.15 Bournemouth W.-Waterloo	34048	WC 4-6-2	397
12.57	12.43	258	9.20 Weymouth-Waterloo	34040	WC 4-6-2	
1.00			Vans to Kensington	30245	M7 0-4-4T	
1.01	1.01	452	12.54 Waterloo-Bournemouth C.	30765	N15 4-6-0	
	12.49	259	10.30 Lymington Pier-Waterloo		Not observed	
1.07	12.58	260	9.25 Sidmouth-Waterloo	73041	5MT 4-6-0	23
1.07	1.07	454	1.00 Waterloo-Plymouth	34050	BB 4-6-2	461
1.08			Down light engine (Central)	30901	V 4-4-0	spl
1.10	1.02	261	10.50 Hinton Admiral-Waterloo	73018	5MT 4-6-0	
1.10	12.51	M162	10.14 Hastings-Sheffield Vic.	31900	U1 2-6-0	
1.12	1.12	455	1.05 Waterloo-Exeter C.	30919	V 4-4-0	10
1.14	1.14s		1.08 Victoria-Tunbridge Wells	80017	4MT 2-6-4T	
1.21		W101/1	10.45 Hastings-Walsall	31867	N 2-6-0	
1.28	1.27s		11.47 Tunbridge Wells-Victoria	42090	4MT 2-6-4T	
1.30	1.29	456	1.22 Waterloo-Bournemouth C.	34094	WC 4-6-2	
1.31	1.24	W101/2	Relief Brighton-Walsall	31891	U1 2-6-0	
1.35	1.20	262	12.12 Basingstoke-Waterloo	30507	S15 4-6-0	107
1.37	1.31	263	9.25 Exmouth-Waterloo	34062	BB 4-6-2	526
1.38	1.37	458	1.30 Waterloo-Weymouth	35024	MN 4-6-2	
1.44	1.35	264	10.40 Bournemouth W.-Waterloo	30791	N15 4-6-0	262
1.45	1.31	457	1.24 Waterloo-Salisbury	30501	N15 4-6-0	
1.49	1.43	265	12.05 Salisbury-Waterloo	30450	N15 4-6-0	
1.50	1.37	M495	10.51 Hastings-Leicester L.Rd.	30915	V 4-4-0	
2.00	1.49	267	9.38 Littleham-Waterloo	34069	BB 4-6-2	537
2.04	2.01	269	8.10 Ilfracombe-Waterloo	35009	MN 4-6-2	
2.06		W941	Relief Brighton-Manchester	34067	BB 4-6-2	spl
2.09	2.07	459	Empty Waterloo-Basingstoke	76025	4MT 2-6-0	
2.09	2.08	270	8.25 Plymouth-Waterloo	35012	MN 4-6-2	9
2.15	2.14s		2.08 Victoria-Tunbridge Wells	31902	U1 2-6-0	
2.17	1.57	268	12.53 Basingstoke-Waterloo	30774	N15 4-6-0	69
2.21	2.27	273	1.08 Andover Jc-Waterloo	31806	U 2-6-0	162
2.24	2.16	271	11.00 Bournemouth W.-Waterloo	35021	MN 4-6-2	388
2.26	2.27s		12.47 Tunbridge Wells-Victoria	80145	4MT 2-6-4T	
2.28	2.19	272	11.43 Lymington Pier-Waterloo	30909	V 4-4-0	24
2.37	2.37	460	2.30 Waterloo-Weymouth	35027	MN 4-6-2	
2.39	2.20	W460	11.05 Walsall-Hastings	34097	WC 4-6-2	
2.41	2.41	461	2.34 Waterloo-Bournemouth W.	30864	LN 4-6-0	392
2.42	2.30	274	9.10 Torrington-Waterloo	73114	5MT 4-6-0	14
2.47	2.33	275	12.10 Bournemouth W.-Waterloo	73117	5MT 4-6-0	41
2.51	2.38	276	11.34 Swanage-Waterloo	34041	WC 4-6-2	398
2.52			Relief Waterloo-Bournemouth C.	34046	WC 4-6-2	
2.57	2.43	277	11.25 Weymouth-Waterloo	35022	MN 4-6-2	383
3.01	3.01	463	2.54 Waterloo-Basingstoke	30796	N15 4-6-0	465
3.02	2.55	W499	12.30 Hastings-Manchester	45426	5MT 4-6-0	LMR
3.07	3.07	464	3.00 Waterloo-Plymouth	35011	MN 4-6-2	
3.07	2.57	278	8.10 Wadebridge-Waterloo	34047	WC 4-6-2	
3.10	3.03	279	9.40 Ilfracombe-Waterloo	73119	5MT 4-6-0	
3.13	3.12	465	3.05 Waterloo-Exeter C.	35008	MN 4-6-2	

4 The West London Lines

The West London Extension Railway was a prolongation of the West London Railway, commencing at a theoretical West London Extension Junction some 34 chains beyond Kensington Addison Road station. Its route followed the course of the Kensington Canal, which was filled in except for the portion at Chelsea between King's Road and the river basin. At Lillie Bridge on the west side of the line, beyond the present Underground depot, there was a group of exchange sidings often used for marshalling trains to and from the southern companies; these finally closed in December 1974. West Brompton was the first of the WLER's passenger stations; it was opened on 1 September 1866, three years before the Metropolitan District built its station alongside. On the other side of the WLER was the LNWR's Brompton & Fulham goods depot.

The next passenger station was at Chelsea & Fulham, opened with the line on 2 March 1863. Beyond the King's Road overbridge was Chelsea Basin signalbox, controlling branches to the Imperial Gasworks and to the sidings serving the riverside wharves and Chelsea dock. Chelsea Basin closed to freight traffic in December 1981, and the site has now been occupied by the luxury development known as Chelsea Harbour. The WLER line then curved to climb up to the bridge over the river at Chelsea, often termed Cremorne Bridge after the former pleasure gardens nearby. The bridge was 1,020ft long and was formed of six cast iron spans over the water and seven shorter approach arches.

The line continued on an embankment past the old village of Battersea to reach the two wooden platforms of Battersea station, also opened on 2 March 1863. Situated beyond Battersea station was the series of Latchmere junctions and their signalbox. First came the No 2 or South Western junction, leading to the Windsor Line side at Clapham Junction; six chains further was the No 1 or Main junction, connecting with the LBSCR at Falcon Junction. Both these lines into Clapham Junction station have already been described. The area between them was formerly occupied by streets of small terrace houses, but war damage and slum clearance have transformed it into a public open space. A short distance beyond

No 1 junction was No 3 junction for a 31 chain curve, which came into use on 6 July 1865, climbing to join the LSWR Windsor Line in the Waterloo direction at West London Junction; railwaymen referred to this as the 'creep-up spur'.

The WLER 'main line' then burrowed beneath the combined tracks of the LSWR and LBSCR routes respectively to Waterloo and Victoria, and after 1866 its passage through this long series of bridges was shared with the LCDR line from Clapham Junction. The parallel WLER and LCDR lines then crossed Pouparts Lane on the level. This crossing was replaced in December 1880 by a footbridge linking the Shaftesbury estate with Culvert Road; the developers of the estate had failed to obtain a station here. The 1867 LBSCR high level route into Victoria crossed the WLER and LCDR lines at this point. The WLER terminated in the Longhedge Junction complex, where the LBSCR's original route from Pouparts Junction joined on the north side and the three incoming routes rearranged themselves into independent LBSCR and LCDR lines to Victoria via Stewarts Lane and a LCDR spur to Factory Junction on its main line to Kent.

As most of the GWR was still being worked on the broad gauge when the WLER was planned, its main line to Victoria and the branch to Falcon Junction were laid with mixed gauge track to accommodate Great Western trains. However, when GWR local trains from Southall began running to Victoria from 1 April 1863, the standard gauge was used. It was only the longer distance services from Windsor or Reading, often detached from Paddington trains at Old Oak Common, which were formed of broad gauge stock, and these ceased in October 1866. The broad gauge continued to be used for goods traffic to Chelsea Basin until November 1875.

The West London and the Extension railways were operated by the trains of the owning companies under the control of a Joint Superintendent at Kensington. This official was initially drawn from either the LNWR or the GWR, but as with maintenance, the Great Western eventually took sole responsibility on behalf of the other companies. As a result, the WLER was controlled from GWR pattern signalboxes — one

of their lower quadrant signals stood close to the Windsor Line at Clapham Junction until recent years. Thus, at nationalisation, the West London lines from Latchmere Junction northwards became part of the Western Region, but from 1 February 1970 they passed to the London Midland Region (at this period Kensington Olympia was the centre of the LMR's Motorail activity). Finally, in April 1988, the whole line was transferred to the Southern Region as part of its overall responsibility for Channel Tunnel works, extending to the planned North Pole rolling stock depot at Old Oak Common.

The spur from Latchmere Junction to West London Junction, which had not seen regular use since 1912, was removed on 21 January 1936 — probably to avoid the expense of installing colour light signalling at the junction. The Victoria resignalling scheme involved some drastic rationalisation in the Longhedge Junction area; the four parallel WLER and LCDR tracks were merged in July 1978 into one double line from a new junction at Culvert Road, while beyond the simplified Longhedge Junction, only a single reversible road led to Stewarts Lane. Chelsea Basin, the only surviving intermediate box on the WLER, was closed in 1982, Latchmere Junction box followed, and on 24 April 1983 the line as far as

Chelsea was brought under the control of the South Eastern panel in the Clapham Junction signalling centre. The down line spur from Latchmere Junction to Clapham Junction Windsor side was then made bi-directional and from 25 May 1990 it became a single line when the up track was taken out of use.

Before the coming of the Underground, the tramcar and the motorbus, the West London lines provided a wide variety of through services for cross-London journeys. When the WLER first opened in 1863, the LBSCR and the LNWR jointly worked a service from Euston to New (East) Croydon via Willesden Junction, Kensington, Clapham Junction and Crystal Palace. The LBSCR ran to West Croydon from Kensington, while the LSWR worked local trains between Clapham Junction and Kensington. The GWR service from Southall to Victoria has already been mentioned.

When the spur to West London Junction was opened in July 1865, a service began from Euston to London Bridge via Willesden Junction, Kensington and the connecting line to the SER at Waterloo. Diverted to Cannon Street in February 1867, it ceased a year later, but was revived between July 1875 and January 1893 as far as Waterloo, with LSWR motive power from Kensington. The newly-opened

Above:
**Stroudley 'D' No B629, on a Kensington to Clapham Junction
train of three ex-LBSCR and two ex-LSWR coaches, leaves
West Brompton on 21 April 1932.**
Ian Allan Library — O.J.Morris

LCDR/LSWR line into Clapham Junction carried from 3 April 1866 a LCDR service to the City as well as LSWR trains to Ludgate Hill. From 1 January 1869 the LNWR began to work its own trains into Victoria, these starting at Broad Street until 1 February 1872, when Willesden Junction became their point of origin. This service survived until 1 October 1917 and then continued for parcels traffic until September 1939. Less enduring was the LNWR's Willesden Junction to Herne Hill service via Factory Junction, which operated between June 1880 and November 1900.

The LSWR's expansion in Middlesex from 1 January 1869 created several new services over the WLER. The first was a Waterloo to Richmond service via West London Junction and Kensington, matched by City trains from Ludgate Hill to Richmond via Factory Junction and Longhedge Junction. Some of the LSWR trains from Clapham Junction to Kensington were subsequently extended to Richmond or Hounslow over the new line.

To summarise the WLER's traffic in April 1887, there were 40 weekday trains between Clapham Junction and Kensington — 35 provided by the LSWR or LBSCR plus five LNWR through trains to Willesden Junction. From Waterloo there were 15 LSWR departures for Richmond and eight LNWR trains to Willes-

den. Victoria despatched nine LNWR trains to Willesden and four GWR ones to Southall. From the Factory Junction direction there were four LNWR Herne Hill to Willesden services and 11 LSWR Ludgate Hill to Richmond workings. Local passenger services had reached their zenith by June 1899, when 94 southbound trains passed Latchmere Junction on weekdays — 45 LSWR, 16 LBSCR, 23 LNWR and 10 GWR. Most of the 26 scheduled freight trains consequently ran at night. Imagination can only wonder at the variety of liveries, motive power and rolling stock which would have been seen passing Latchmere Junction at that period.

Competition from other forms of transport soon began to have its effect on the West London, however. August 1908 saw 24 LBSCR trains from Clapham Junction to Kensington, plus 21 LSWR ones, of which 13 continued via Gunnersbury to Twicken-

Above:
A GWR South Lambeth to Acton freight train passes West Brompton station of the West London Extension Railway (per the nameboard), double-headed by pannier tanks Nos 8700 and 5727, on 28 August 1933. A District Line train can just be seen in the LPTB station alongside.
Ian Allan Library — H.C.Casserley

Below:
The Lillie Bridge to Peckham Rye coal train waits behind 'E6x' 0-6-2T No 2411 at Clapham Junction, c1947, to get the road out of the West London platform.
Lens of Sutton

ham. On weekdays each company despatched its trains from its own platforms at Clapham Junction, but on Sundays a joint service was operated on alternate weeks by each company from its usual platform — passengers who mistook the date might have to make a lengthy dash along the footbridge! This confusion was ended by the withdrawal of Sunday services in May 1918. In addition to the LSWR/LBSCR service, there were five LNWR trains making the Croydon-Willesden journey.

From Waterloo there were 14 weekday and 10 Sunday trains to Richmond via Kensington, but this service was already languishing, and the coal strike of 1912 offered the opportunity to withdraw it from 12 March. Victoria had 10 LNWR departures and nine GWR ones, the latter company also running three Sunday trains, including two rail motors to Greenford. Although the LSWR Ludgate Hill to Richmond service was suffering from the competition of the District's electric trains, 10 trains daily were still running, though numbers were soon reduced prior to their final withdrawal in 1915. The SECR (former LCDR) trains to Clapham Junction also dwindled, and ceased altogether from 3 April 1916. GWR trains to Victoria were withdrawn from 22 May 1915, and the LSWR service beyond Kensington on the line to Richmond finished on 5 June 1916. The exigencies of war thus brought to an end little-used services which had become relics of the Victorian era in London's transport facilities.

Of all the local services which had used the WLER, only the Clapham Junction to Kensington trains remained at the return of peace. For a time these did not run during the middle of the day, and, although about 30 trains each way ran on weekdays, the service never regained its prewar all-day frequency. Grouping brought little change to the service: ex-LSWR 0-4-4Ts from Nine Elms worked the trains starting from platform 1 at Clapham Junction, while a Marsh 4-4-2T or even a Stroudley 'D' tank might appear on those leaving from platform 12. Exhibitions and circuses at Olympia brought additional traffic, while Chelsea football ground was close enough to be served by Chelsea & Fulham station. For example, on Easter Monday 1939, Chelsea was at home to Charlton, and a five-minute interval service was provided from Clapham Junction, using the two regular train sets and three extra formations; in addition, through excursions arrived from Erith and Plumstead.

Below:
A Clapham Junction to Kensington van train passes the still largely intact buildings of Chelsea & Fulham station on 27 May 1950. 'M7' 0-4-4T No 30038 was one of the locos painted in malachite green to bring a splash of colour to the Clapham to Waterloo empty stock workings.
Ian Allan Library — E.R.Wethersett/LPC

As well as the SR service, there were occasional LMS trains from Willesden to Clapham Junction and East Croydon via Crystal Palace. The Croydon passenger service ceased in March 1929, but continued as a parcels working during the summer, and at other times when required for 'Passengers Luggage in Advance' traffic. The LMS passenger train to Clapham Junction was withdrawn in October 1940, but the parcels working to Croydon continued until the 1960s — by then with diesel traction rather than a Webb 0-6-2T or a Fowler 2-6-2T. The GWR also ran to Clapham Junction between 1924 and 1938 with a workmens' service from Greenford.

The outbreak of war in September 1939 saw the WLER service reduced to 12 trains each way during peak hours only, thus freeing the line for the movement of freight and military traffic. Enemy bombing during 1940 destroyed Battersea station and seriously damaged West Brompton and Kensington Addison Road. The advertised train service was withdrawn from 21 October 1940, but two non-stop trains daily in each direction still ran between Clapham Junction and Kensington for the benefit of staff at the offices of the Post Office Savings Bank. These trains reappeared in the public timetable between 18 June 1951 and 11 June 1956, when the prospect of the POSB's move to Glasgow cast a doubt over the future of the service. However, other office development in the neighbourhood of Kensington Olympia station maintained the faithful band of commuters using the service, and its existence was once again publicly acknowledged from 5 May 1969. With patronage increasing, a much improved service of four return trips in the morning and four in the evening was introduced from 16 May 1983. Further additions have swelled the local service to 11 trains each way on Mondays to Fridays in the 1990-91 timetable.

Motive power and rolling stock has been varied on the 'Kenny Belle' — to give the train its unofficial title. It was the last steam-worked suburban service in London; ex-SECR 'H' class 0-4-4Ts and BR Standard or LMS design 2-6-2Ts were succeeded from July 1967 by Class 33 diesels. Formations have often been unusual — for example, with the ex-SECR converted rail motor set used in the mid-1950s, and BR's only plastic bodied carriage included during the final days of steam. The variety continued with diesel traction — a couple of Mk 1 coaches or a push-pull set, including one converted from 4-COR electric stock.

Right:
Stanier '8F' 2-8-0 No 48666 brings a Willesden to Norwood freight up the sharp curve into platform 17 at Clapham Junction on 20 July 1951. Construction of the new power box obscures the view of the LBSCR-built 'B' cabin, while a concrete gantry has been erected to carry colour light starting signals for the West London platforms.
Brian Morrison

Subsequently, the augmented 1983 service was worked in the morning by a WR Cross-Country Class 119 DMU (off the Gatwick-Reading service) and in the evening by a Class 33/1 diesel and a 4-TC push-pull set, which went on to form a train to Salisbury. During the summer of 1989 Class 73 electro-diesels provided the motive power; however, while their 600hp diesel motors were adequate to haul a TC set, they could not heat it during the winter, so they were replaced by a variety of suburban DMUs supplied from Old Oak Common by the WR. The Solent electrification in May 1990 made available a SR Class 205 or 207 DEMU which arrived each morning from Eastleigh to operate the service.

The West London line offered a solution to the problem of crossing London for Victorian and Edwardian travellers with their mounds of luggage. As early as 1864 there had been a broad-gauge slip coach from Bristol to Victoria. This had a successor in 1905-06

when a Birkenhead to Dover through coach was slipped at Southall and taken into Victoria. At the turn of the century the LNWR had through coaches from Birmingham via Willesden Junction and Herne Hill to Dover and to Queenborough (for Flushing). A choice of London terminal was offered by the LBSCR's Paddington to Brighton service of 1906-07 and by an LNWR train from Victoria to Wolverhampton between October 1910 and December 1912.

The best known of the through services over the West London line was the 'Sunny South Express', introduced in July 1904 to link Liverpool, Manchester and Birmingham with Brighton and Eastbourne; in 1905 Dover and Deal were added to its destinations. The LNWR provided corridor and dining car stock for the train (the LBSCR had none of its own), but the latter company hauled it from Willesden. Withdrawn during World War 1, the 'Sunny South' was restored by stages in 1921-22 and under LMS

The 10.51am Hastings-Leicester approaches Clapham Junction on 25 August 1956, hauled by Atlantic No 32425 *Trevose Head*. Somewhere in the LMR, a non-corridor brake second of LMS design has replaced a Maunsell corridor brake in the train's formation. *Author*

The driver of Class 5 4-6-0 No 44937 is leaning out of his cab to catch sight through Freemasons Bridge of the signal for the divergence to the West London line. The 12.30pm Hastings-Manchester was a LMR loco working from Brighton northwards. Also in the photograph on 31 August 1957, the retaining wall of New Wandsworth goods yard was being strengthened; most of it has now disappeared. *Author*

auspices acquired a Sheffield portion from 1925. The
service ran daily in the summer, expanding into several portions on Saturdays, but operated only at
weekends during the winter; advertised stops were
made at Willesden Junction, where the Kent portion
was detached, and at Kensington Addison Road.

War in September 1939 once again ended the service and it was not until the summer of 1949 that
through trains to the South Coast were resumed at
weekends only. Services included Walsall and Birmingham to Brighton and Hastings, Leicester to Hastings via Northampton and, from 1950, a Friday
overnight train from Manchester to Eastbourne and
Hastings, returning on Saturday afternoon, which
was worked through to and from Brighton by an LMR
Class 5 4-6-0. Although most WR trains from the Midlands to the South Coast ran via Reading and Redhill,

some Saturday extras ran via High Wycombe and the
West London line to resorts in both Sussex and
Thanet. This route was also used during 1965-66 to
relieve the West Coast main line during
electrification. The 1950s saw the introduction of Saturday through trains off the Great Central line to the
South Coast, some of them from such unusual starting points as Derby Friargate and Mansfield Central.
GC line trains, and those off the WR, usually made an
unadvertised stop at Kensington to change engines;
the SR then provided a rich variety of motive power

Below:
**The Croydon-Wood Lane milk train has a minimal load as it
approaches the junction for the West London line on 16 May
1959 behind ex-LBSCR 'C2x' 0-6-0 No 32547.** *Author*

Above:
The 'Midlands-Merseyman' was a through freight service from Brighton to the LMR introduced during the 1960s. Passing New Wandsworth on 15 May 1964, its long train was in the charge of No D6541, now renumbered 33023.
Ian Allan Library — Brian Stephenson

to work these through trains between Willesden or Kensington and the coast.

The run-down of the GC main line resulted in the transfer to the Midland line in 1965 of the Ramsgate to Nottingham and Derby trains, now hauled by 'Peak' class diesels. This now brought them through Clapham Junction station on the Windsor Line side en route from Longhedge Junction via New Kew Junction to the Midland Main Line at Brent. These connections on the LSWR side at Clapham Junction have always seen less through traffic than those on the Brighton side. Between 1905 and 1910 there was a service from Weymouth and Bournemouth to Liverpool or Manchester, with carriages for Kings Cross going forward via Ludgate Hill and the Widened Lines. The LSWR itself ran a circuitous train during 1907-08 from Richmond (New) via Hammersmith, Kensington, Clapham Junction and Wimbledon to Salisbury to enable residents of West London to reach the West Country without changing.

In more recent years there have been various short-lived through workings off the West London line; a

Coventry to Bournemouth train in 1929-33, a Manchester to Weymouth service in 1970 and a curious Bolton-Preston-Poole train in 1988, all running on summer Saturdays only. The Clapham Junction to Longhedge Junction connection was used during the 1930s by steam trains from Kingston to Ramsgate and in 1985 by an electric from Reading to Folkestone, but these were really timetabled excursions.

By the 1970s, most of these weekend through trains had ceased as holidaymakers deserted the South Coast beaches for Mediterranean sun. However, this created traffic at Gatwick Airport and encouraged the idea of direct services from the Midlands and North of England. From 14 May 1979, two trains daily were

Top:
**A Hither Green to Old Oak Common freight passes the site
of the future Culvert Road Junction on 29 January 1966,
hauled by No D6519 (later to become No 33106). A train
from Horsham and Gatwick Airport crosses the viaduct
above, on its way to Victoria.** *Author*

Above:
**The 08.45 Reading to Eastbourne excursion comes off the
West London line on 10 April 1966. Its formation of three-
car, three-car and four-car DMUs would not provide access
to toilets for many of its passengers, thus maintaining the
traditional rigours of excursion travel.** *Author*

introduced between Manchester, Birmingham, Oxford, Gatwick and Brighton; these had no public stops between Reading and East Croydon, being worked through by WR Class 47 diesel locos.

Their success led the newly-formed InterCity sector to expand the through services over the West London line from 12 May 1986. On weekdays, seven trains ran from Manchester or Liverpool — three to Brighton, one to Newhaven and three to Dover Western Docks. All of them called at Kensington Olympia (which was refurbished as an InterCity station) and those bound for Brighton or Newhaven served Clapham Junction. There were even five trains each way on Sundays, thus providing a sabbath service from Clapham to Kensington for the first time since 1918. The route to the north was over the WCML, usually via the Trent Valley, so that Oxford lost all and Birmingham most of their through services to Gatwick.

In 1988 there was a complete reappraisal of the services offered, and from 16 May there was a return to the Thames Valley route by the three trains remaining. One of these continued to serve Kent (maintaining a once daily passenger train between Latchmere Junction and Factory Junction), but now ran to Dover Priory and Folkestone. The two others went to Gatwick and Brighton, but terminated instead at Eastbourne on summer Saturdays. From May 1989 the morning service from Brighton was diverted from

Manchester to run to Glasgow, under the title of the 'Sussex Scot'. The recital of the 17 stops made by this train after leaving Clapham Junction makes an unexpected break from the announcements on platforms 15 and 16 of South London destinations.

Kensington Olympia became after 1965 the home of London's Motorail services, but the West London line had already seen the passage of many previous car-carrying trains. Dover and its Channel ferries was the destination of trains from Manchester Central, Newton-le-Willows, Stockton, Stirling and York at various times between 1956 and 1979, almost all being overnight services. Clapham Junction saw Motorail trains from 1958, originally a Glasgow St Enoch to Eastbourne service, but later running from Stirling to Newhaven, until it ceased in 1969.

Besides the timetabled services described, the West London line has always seen many special trains. At weekends, frequent excursions off the GWR and LMS

Above:
The 'Kenny Belle' stands at Kensington Olympia on 5 May 1970, formed of push-pull Class 33 loco No 6538 (No 33118) and set No 601 converted from 4-COR electric stock. Unfortunately this set, No 601, was damaged beyond repair in a collision. *Author*

systems, from stations as far out as Oxford or Rugby, ran to the whole gamut of seaside resorts in Sussex and Kent. With steam traction, ex-LMS engines could work through to most destinations, but ex-GWR types had to be replaced by SR locos at Kensington. Other excursions came from Bedford and intermediate stations on the Midland main line via Kew and called at Clapham Junction on the Windsor side to change engines or train crews. The coming of diesel railcars in the late 1950s simplified the working of excursion trains off the WR, with some long and varied formations appearing. There were fewer attractions for northbound excursions from the SR until the 'Merrymaker' promotions of the 1970s explored a wide variety of unusual destinations.

If the cheap trip excursion train is almost extinct, up-market traffic has been catered for in recent years by the VSOE Pullman train with regular tours from Victoria to Bath and Bristol, either via the West London line and Newbury or via Clapham Junction, Chertsey and Salisbury. In addition VSOE charter trains have been run frequently to race meetings or

for private parties; with Victoria the usual starting point, their patrons have the opportunity of the Pullman's leisurely progress to enjoy the scenery of the Longhedge area and of the West London Extension line.

Activities at Olympia and Earls Court, such as Bertram Mills circus, the Motor Show and the former British Industries Fair, brought special trains to the West London lines carrying visitors, animals and exhibits. The Royal Tournament and any major ceremonial occasion in London involving military participation saw troop trains arriving at Kensington Addison Road, where the wide platforms and numerous bays provided suitable unloading facilities for horses, guns and vehicles. Additionally, London Territorial Army units bound for their annual training camp would often leave from Kensington. The location of large Army bases at Aldershot, Shorncliffe and on Salisbury Plain meant that most of these specials would travel over the SR, many of them through Clapham Junction.

These peacetime exercises were only a prelude to the military movements over the West London lines during the two world wars. In 1917, military traffic through Kensington averaged a score of trains daily, which paused at Lillie Bridge yard to change over to SECR or LBSCR motive power. The most intensive periods of traffic were during the initial mobilisation and despatch of the BEF to France in August 1914, which involved some cancellation of civilian passen-

Below:
This view taken on 28 September 1979 shows the newly established convergence of the Clapham Junction and the West London Extension lines at Culvert Road Junction, with No 73103 approaching on the Clapham Junction to Stewarts Lane empty stock transfer working. *Author*

Bottom:
The 08.12 to Kensington leaves platform 2 at Clapham Junction on 20 August 1982, its two Mk 1 coaches hauled by No 73142 *Broadlands*, resplendent for its next duty on the VSOE Pullman. *Ian Allan Library — J.Scrace*

ger services, and following the evacuation from Dunkerque in May and June 1940.

One of the principal objects of the West London lines was the direct movement of freight to and from the railways south of the Thames. A steady stream of goods trains had to be fitted in between the regular passenger services using Kensington in the years between the wars. The SR, anxious to avoid any delay to its commuter traffic, would not accept freight trains at Clapham Junction between 6.20am and 9.50am or 4.00pm and 7.20pm, so that any late-running goods off the West London had then to be impounded in Lillie Bridge sidings. Even as late as 1954, of the 61 southbound weekday trains over the WLER, 43 were freight. The others comprised four passenger or empty coach workings, seven milk trains and seven conveying parcels or 'horse & carriage' traffic. Of the 43 freight trains, 11 were worked by the LMR, seven were WR services to their depots at South Lambeth and Chelsea Basin, the ER had four Temple Mills to Hither Green trips, while the SR operated 21 trains from Willesden, Old Oak Common and Lillie Bridge to its marshalling yards at Norwood Junction and Hither Green as well as to smaller local depots. The Maunsell 'W' class 2-6-4Ts handled much of this cross-London traffic.

Much of this freight activity arose from the movement of domestic coal bound for the homes of South East England. However, the coming of central heating as well as the decline in general merchandise wagonload business has caused this pattern of traffic to disappear almost completely. Marshalling yards, local coal sidings and even major goods depots, such as South Lambeth, have closed as the freight traffic over the West London has become concentrated on bulk (often one-company) trainloads.

The West London lines and associated running powers enabled the northern companies to establish freight and coal depots south of the river. In the Clapham area, the GWR had its large all-purpose depot at South Lambeth, the Midland had a yard nearby at Wandsworth Road, while the LNWR owned Clapham Junction's second local goods yard at Falcon Lane. This mainly handled domestic coal, but also served several private traders' premises, including the United Glass Bottle Manufacturers Ltd. For many years a LMS Class 4F 0-6-0 was a familiar sight at work in this yard, which opened on 1 June 1869 and closed 99 years later on 3 June 1968. Part of the site is now occupied by the black, fortress-like building of the Clapham Junction signalling centre, the rest by a large supermarket.

Right:
The 'Sussex Scot', the 09.18 Brighton-Glasgow, approaches Clapham Junction cautiously on the slow line. It is headed by No 47825 *Thomas Telford*, 24 August 1990. *C.J.Marsden*

Above:
No 33055 passes the LT Lillie Bridge depot on the Dundee to Dover Speedlink service on 14 May 1986, with the office blocks near Kensington Olympia station in the background.
C.J.Marsden

Below:
In Railfreight livery, No 47156 heads a train of logs bound for the West London line near New Wandsworth on 13 April 1989. A winter formation 'Gatwick Express' passes in the opposite direction, 13 April 1989. *C.J.Marsden*

The Passing Scene — Wednesday 26 September 1990

(Down trains only)

Time	Line	Train	Headcode	Stock	Loco
17.00s	MS	16.52 Waterloo-Farnham	53	CIG/VEP	
17.01s	WF	16.56 Waterloo-Richmond-Shepperton	(47)	455	
17.01	MF	16.55 Waterloo-Portsmouth & Southsea	72	CIG	
17.02s	MS	16.35 Waterloo-Chessington S.(20m late)	(18)	2x455	
17.02s	CS	16.55 Victoria-Horsham	84	2x4EPB	
17.05s	MS	16.55 Waterloo-Hampton Court	(30)	455	
17.05	CF	17.00 Victoria-Gatwick Airport	20	G.Exp(8)	73135
17.06	MF	17.00 Waterloo-Eastleigh-Portsmouth Hbr	80	VEP	
17.06	WS	17.00 Waterloo-Reading via Hounslow	37	VEP	
17.07s	CS	17.00 Victoria-W.Croydon-Epsom Downs	92	4 EPB/2EPB	
17.07	CF	17.02 Victoria-Uckfield	88	2x205 (DEMU)	
17.08	MF	17.02 Waterloo-Southampton	93	CIG/VEP	
17.10s	CF	17.04 Victoria-Tattenham Corner	(74)	455	
17.11s	MS	17.03 Waterloo-Kingston-Shepperton	(24)	2x455	
17.11	MF	17.05 Waterloo-Exeter St. Davids		9xMk2	50049
17.13s	CF	17.07 Victoria-Brighton	14	3xCIG	
17.13s	MS	17.01 Waterloo-Cobham-Guildford	(42)	2x455	
17.14s	WF	17.05 Waterloo-Brentford-Hounslow Loop	(89)	455	
17.15	MF	17.08 Waterloo-Portsmouth Hbr.	82	VEP/HAP	
17.15s	CS	17.05 Victoria-Crystal Palace-W.Croydon	94	2x319	
17.16s	MS	17.05 Waterloo-Chessington South	(18)	2x455	
17.17	MF	17.10 Waterloo-Guildford	75	VEP/2xHAP	
17.17a	2	17.03 Kensington (O)-Clapham Junction	(20)	205 (DEMU)	
17.17s	WS	17.10 Waterloo-Ascot-Guildford	28	VEP/HAP	
17.18s	MS	17.10 Waterloo-Epsom-Effingham Junction	(16)	2x455	
17.18	CF	17.09 Victoria-Brighton	44	4EPB/VEP	
17.20s	CS	17.13 Victoria-Epsom	84	4EPB/2EPB	
17.20	CF	17.15 Victoria-Gatwick Airport	30	G.Exp(8)	73207
17.21s	WF	17.12 Waterloo-Windsor	(58)	455	
17.22s	CS	17.15 Victoria-Selhurst	(02)	2x455	
17.22	MF	17.15 Waterloo-Weymouth	(91)	2x442	
17.23s	CF	17.17 Victoria-Seaford/Eastbourne	52	3xCIG	
17.24s	WF	17.15 Waterloo-Richmond-Kingston Loop	(32)	2x455	
17.25	MF	17.18 Waterloo-Alton	51	2xVEP	
17.27s	MS	17.17 Waterloo-Kingston-Richmond Loop	(21)	2x455	
17.27	MF	17.20 Waterloo-Havant-Southampton	5	HAP/VEP	
17.27	WS	17.20 Waterloo-Reading	36	2xVEP	
17.28s	CS	17.20 Victoria-Beckenham Junction	86	2x4EPB	
17.28s	CF	17.23 Victoria-Southampton/Littlehampton	46	CIG/BIG/CIG	
17.29	MF	17.22 Waterloo-Cobham-Guildford	(42)	2x455	
17.29s	MS	17.20 Waterloo-Dorking	(17)	2x455	
17.31	MF	17.24 Waterloo-Eastleigh	93	VEP/CIG/HAP	
17.32s	CS	17.25 Victoria-Horsham	84	2x4EPB	
17.33s	MS	17.25 Waterloo-Hampton Court	(30)	2x455	
17.33	MF	17.26 Waterloo-Farnham	52	VEP/2xHAP	
17.35	CF	17.21 Victoria-Bognor Regis (8m late)	6	CIG/BIG/CIG	
17.36s	WS	17.30 Waterloo-Ascot-Guildford	28	VEP	
17.37	MF	17.30 Waterloo-Bournemouth/Fareham	92	2x6REP	
17.37	CF	17.30 Victoria-Gatwick Airport	20	G.Exp(8)	73210
17.37s	CS	17.30 Victoria-W.Croydon-Epsom Downs	92	2x4EPB	
17.37a	2	17.27 Kensington (O)-Clapham Jc	(20)	205 (DEMU)	
17.38s	MS	17.30 Waterloo-Dorking	(17)	2x455	
17.39	MF	17.32 Waterloo-Portsmouth Hbr.	81	HAP/2xVEP	
17.39	CF	17.32 Victoria-East Grinstead	66	2x2EPB/VEP	
17.41s	CF	17.34 Victoria-Smitham	(74)	455	

Time	Line	Train	Headcode	Stock	Loco
17.41s	WF	17.26 Waterloo-Richmond-Shepperton	(47)	2x455	
17.42s	CS	17.35 Victoria-Crystal Palace-W.Croydon	94	319	
17.42	MF	17.34 Waterloo-Yeovil Junction		6xMk2	50029
17.44s	CF	17.36 Victoria-Brighton	14	BIG/CIG/CIG	
17.44	MF	17.36 Waterloo-Basingstoke	63	CIG/VEP	
17.46s	CF	17.40 Victoria-Three Bridges/Reigate	44	2xVEP	
17.46s	WF	17.35 Waterloo-Brentford-Hounslow Loop	(89)	2x455	
17.47s	MS	17.35 Waterloo-Chessington South	(18)	2x455	
17.47	MF	17.38 Waterloo-Cobham-Guildford	(42)	2x455	
17.48s	WS	17.40 Waterloo-Reading via Hounslow	37	VEP/HAP	
17.49s	CS	17.43 Victoria-Epsom	84	2x4EPB	
17.50	CF	17.45 Victoria-Gatwick Airport	30	G.Exp(8)	7320x
17.50	MF	17.40 Waterloo-Portsmouth & Southsea	72	HAP/VEP	
17.52s	WF	17.42 Waterloo-Windsor	(58)	2x455	
17.53s	CS	17.45 Victoria-Selhurst	(02)	2x455	
17.53	MF	17.45 Waterloo-Weymouth	(92)	2x442	
17.54s	CF	17.47 Victoria-Bognor Regis	6	2xCIG	
17.55s	WF	17.45 Waterloo-Richmond-Kingston Loop	(32)	2x455	
17.55	MF	17.48 Waterloo-Alton	51	2xVEP	
17.56s	CS	17.50 Victoria-Beckenham Junction	86	2x4EPB	
17.57	CF	17.51 Victoria-Eastbourne	50	BIG/CIG/CIG	
17.58	MF	17.50 Waterloo-Cobham-Guildford	(42)	2x455	
17.58s	MS	17.47 Waterloo-Kingston-Richmond Loop	(21)	2x455	
17.59s	WS	17.50 Waterloo-Ascot-Aldershot	28	HAP/CIG	

Notes:

s = Train stopping at Clapham Junction

Lines:
WF	South Western Windsor Fast	
WS	South Western Windsor Slow	
MF	South Western Main Fast	
MS	South Western Main Slow	
CF	Central Lines Fast	
CS	Central Lines Slow	
2	Platform 2 — Kensington service	

Headcodes in brackets were not carried.

Below:
The entrance to the shopping precinct and Clapham Junction station on 3 September 1991. *Brian Morrison*

5 Clapham Junction — Today and Tomorrow

What does 'Britain's Busiest Railway Station' amount to in terms of traffic? In the 1990-91 timetable, Clapham Junction saw approximately 2,250 trains of all descriptions on a normal weekday, rather less on Saturdays and much fewer on Sundays. In comparison, a figure of 2,400 trains per day was quoted in 1919 and 2,550 (exclusive of empty stock movements) in 1939. This decrease has been due to several factors: the loss of much of the railways' freight traffic, with only about a score of trains passing through Clapham Junction on any given day, and the withdrawal of local passenger services, completely on such routes as Waterloo to Wimbledon via East Putney and the Victoria to London Bridge circles, or partially on the West London Extension line and the Kingston and Hounslow loops. There has also been the general reduction in suburban services outside the peak hours from 20-minute to half hourly frequency.

Even the rush hours have seen the discontinuance of many short distance trains — for example Victoria to Streatham Hill and Waterloo to Strawberry Hill. And innovations introduced with timetable changes have been short-lived: the Waterloo to Epsom line used to have semi-fast trains running every 10 minutes in advance of the stopping service, but now only the latter remain, while most of the peak-hour extras to Smitham to compensate for the closure of Coulsdon North have ceased to run. Throughout the 1970s and 1980s the Southern Region has suffered from recurrent shortages of train crews or rolling stock, and therefore these extra peak hour trains have usually been the choice for temporary cancellation, often followed by permanent withdrawal in the next timetable. The introduction of Driver-Only Operation in 1989 on many of the Central routes relieved the situation there, but delays in the extension of the scheme to the South Western sector caused extensive cancellations during 1990 and 1991. With few inner suburban 'extras' remaining these advertised cuts had to be applied to core services resulting in hour-long gaps on some routes — and even with these planned cuts additional short notice cancellations still took place.

On the positive side, there has been the extension of electrification, encouraging commuters to move out into the countryside and swell the SR's longer distance residential traffic, which has been relatively immune from the service reductions and has shown steady growth. Also, the introduction of the 'Gatwick Express' service has created 138 additional trains daily through Clapham Junction.

Taking the 1990-91 timetable as the basis, the Monday to Friday traffic through Clapham Junction divided as follows: South Western passenger 1,185 trains, Central passenger 815, West London passenger 26, South Western empty stock 157, Central empties 45, freight trains between 20 and 25.

Peak hour traffic leaving the London termini between 17.00 and 18.00 has evolved over the years as follows:

	1922	1939	1960	1975	1990
SW-Windsor Line	18	21	18	19	16
SW-fast line	12	16	18	24	23
SW-slow line	12	18	18	23	14
Central-fast line	8	9	16	18	18
Central-slow line	11	17	17	17	12
West London	2	3	2	1	3
Total	63	84	89	102	86

The Windsor Line services above have not been divided between fast and slow roads, as the usual practice is for the stopping trains to take the fast lines between Queenstown Road and Barnes (through platforms 4 and 5 at Clapham Junction) in order to concentrate station working on the island platforms at Wandsworth Town, Putney and Barnes. The slow lines are normally used by the outer suburban services to Reading and Camberley, all of which call at Clapham Junction except for a few during the rush hours.

On the South Western main line, the only trains during the off-peak hours not stopping at Clapham Junction are the Network Expresses to Exeter and Weymouth and the fast trains to Portsmouth Harbour via Guildford. Motive power problems on the West of England line resulted in the cancellation from Jan-

Left:

**Newly-introduced Class 442 'Wessex Electric' stock forms
the 12.30 Waterloo to Weymouth train approaching
Clapham Junction on 23 July 1988. Running parallel on the
down Windsor local line is a fast train for Guildford via
Ascot formed of 4-CIG units.**
Ian Allan Library — J.S.Whiteley

Below left:

**With the end of diesel traction to East Grinstead
approaching, a scratch formation of units Nos 205.007 (with
Hastings motor coach) and 207.003 form a combined East
Grinstead and Uckfield to Victoria service on 2 May 1987.
The train is passing under Boutflower Road bridge, one of
Clapham Junction's vantage points for photographers. On
the left can be seen the retaining wall in front of the Peabody
Trust estate, which had to be cut back in 1981.**
Ian Allan Library — Brian Morrison

uary 1991 of most of the Salisbury semi-fasts which
called at Clapham Junction, and their restoration will
have to await the introduction of Class 159 Express
diesel units in 1992. However, no main line trains
call at Clapham Junction during the busiest period of
the peak hours, thus there were no down services
between 16.59 and 18.10.

The abolition of the Southern Region from April
1991 and its replacement by three divisions within
Network SouthEast, each fully responsible for operating, commercial policy and profitability, has required
some rationalisation of management boundaries. The
Epsom and Leatherhead area has enjoyed through
services to both Waterloo and Victoria since the days
of LSWR and LBSCR joint ownership. Under the new

structure off-peak Waterloo trains terminate at
Epsom, connecting there with South Central Division
trains to Dorking and beyond and Thameslink Line
services towards Effingham Junction. The habits of
the peak-hour commuters may not be so easily
altered to suit management convenience. Another
1991 development on the South West lines was the
restoration of the off-peak service around the
Kingston Roundabout, thanks to a financial contribution from Kingston Corporation concerned about the
poor train service to the town's expanding shopping
facilities.

To turn to the South Central Division lines,
Clapham Junction is served by all main-line off-peak
trains from Victoria with the exception of the four-times-per-hour 'Gatwick Expresses' and the hourly
fast train to Brighton. Since 1990 it has been possible
to travel direct from platform 13 to Southampton via
Hove as an alternative to the Waterloo trains from
platform 9. In contrast to the South Western side,
most of the peak hour main line trains call at
Clapham Junction to pick up passengers, despite the
need to leave paths for the Gatwick Expresses. The
only exceptions during 1990-91 were three main line
departures and the four trains for the Oxted line, but
connections into these could usually be made at East
Croydon. Sunday and Bank Holiday services on the
SR have been reduced considerably in recent years,
and nowhere has the change been more marked than
on the Brighton main line. Instead of a regular interval service augmented by relief and excursion trains,
for most of the year from Victoria to Brighton there is
now only an hourly train calling at all stations
beyond Gatwick — even this is liable to diversion or
partial bus substitution for engineering works.

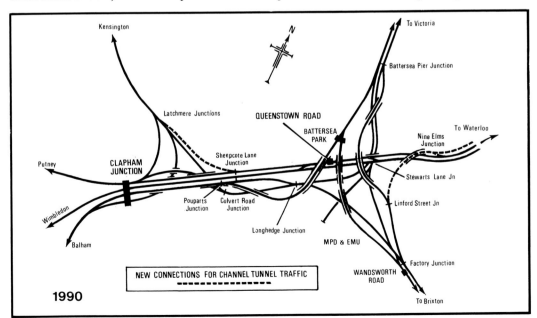

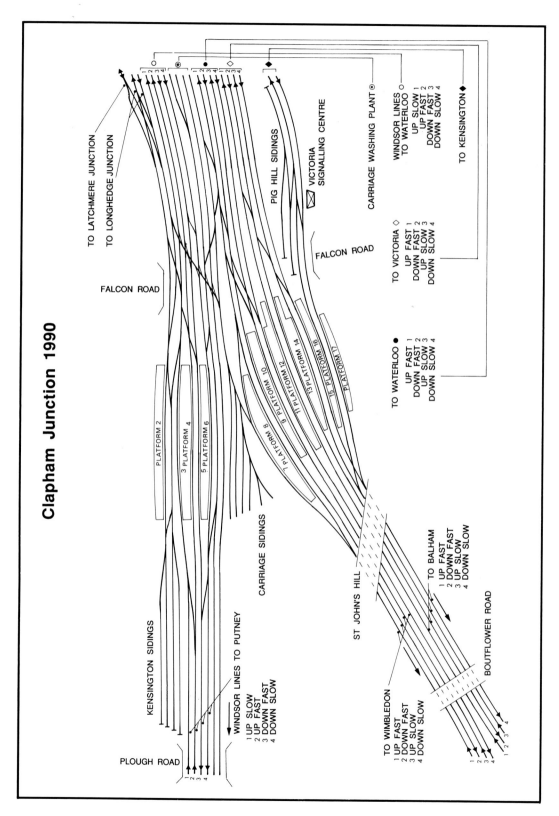

Clapham Junction 1990

TO LATCHMERE JUNCTION

TO LONGHEDGE JUNCTION

FALCON ROAD

FALCON ROAD

PIG HILL SIDINGS

VICTORIA
SIGNALLING CENTRE

CARRIAGE WASHING PLANT ◉

WINDSOR LINES
TO WATERLOO ○
UP SLOW 1
UP FAST 2
DOWN FAST 3
DOWN SLOW 4

TO KENSINGTON ◆

TO VICTORIA ◇
UP FAST 1
DOWN FAST 2
UP SLOW 3
DOWN SLOW 4

TO WATERLOO ●
UP FAST 1
DOWN FAST 2
UP SLOW 3
DOWN SLOW 4

PLATFORM 2

3 PLATFORM 4

5 PLATFORM 6

7 PLATFORM 8

9 PLATFORM 10

11 PLATFORM 12

13 PLATFORM 14

15 PLATFORM 16

PLATFORM 17

CARRIAGE SIDINGS

ST JOHN'S HILL

TO BALHAM
1 UP FAST
2 DOWN FAST
3 UP SLOW
4 DOWN SLOW

BOUTFLOWER ROAD

KENSINGTON SIDINGS

WINDSOR LINES TO PUTNEY

1 UP SLOW
2 UP FAST
3 DOWN FAST
4 DOWN SLOW

TO WIMBLEDON
1 UP FAST
2 DOWN FAST
3 UP SLOW
4 DOWN SLOW

PLOUGH ROAD

1
2
3
4

1
2
3
4

While Clapham Junction has lost some of its originating traffic since 1945, the station has become a major focus for interchange between the South Western and Central routes. The Southern Railway had offered Waterloo and Victoria as alternative destinations on tickets to London from suburban stations. For some years British Railways withdrew this facility, but the more recent policy of issuing tickets to 'London Brit Rail' has encouraged the customers to use the terminal most convenient to themselves. Victoria, once the station for aristocratic Belgravia and the affluent West End, has become surrounded and surmounted by office blocks, while the Victoria Line has brought direct access to much of Central London. In the opposite direction, Croydon has become a major centre for commercial development, and other out of town office building has taken place at Sutton, Wimbledon and Woking. For more distant travel, Gatwick Airport offers a gateway to the world, and its adjacent station is linked to Clapham Junction by six trains hourly.

The range of services now calling at Clapham Junction enables all these possibilities of interchange to be realised during the off-peak hours. However, the absence of peak hour stops by main line trains to and from Waterloo creates difficulties for commuters from outer suburban stations on the South Western section trying to reach Victoria. To take two typical dormitory villages: in 1990-91 a passenger to Wivelsfield

(41 miles) could leave Waterloo at 17.10 and with one change at Clapham Junction arrive at their destination at 18.07. Their counterpart living at Winchfield (40 miles) leaving Victoria at 17.20 had to change at Clapham Junction, Surbiton and Woking before reaching Winchfield at 18.56 — but they could arrive by the same train if they stayed at Victoria until 18.00 and caught it at Clapham Junction at 18.10.

With 23 trains using the fast line out of Waterloo between 17.00 and 18.00, the track was being worked to its capacity and no stops at Clapham Junction could be inserted. On the other hand, the withdrawal of many inner suburban services had left only 14 trains using the slow line. It is unlikely that these trains will ever be restored (some of them were withdrawn a decade ago), so the imbalance can only be adjusted by diverting some services from the fast line and here the prime candidates are those Guildford via Cobham trains at this time which still travel

down the fast line non-stop to Surbiton. If they ran on the slow line they could call at Clapham Junction themselves and also provide gaps on the fast line to allow some main line services to stop; in 1990/91 only the half-hourly Hampton Court trains linked Clapham with the outer suburban area during the busiest part of the rush hour.

Until the abolition of the Southern Region on 1 April 1991, Clapham Junction station (both South Western and Central sides), together with the West London line to Kensington Olympia, came under the control of the Area Manager at Waterloo. The rest of the South Western suburban system formed the Feltham area, while the Victoria area comprised the Central suburban lines (excluding Clapham Junction itself) corresponding to the operating radius of the Central panel in the signalling centre.

Currently 89 staff are employed at Clapham Junction station and yard — a considerable decrease on the 400 people working there for the two pre-Group companies and for the Southern Railway. The LSWR alone employed 120 platform and booking office staff in 1921, but since then most of the ticket offices and barriers have been removed and there is no longer any milk or parcels traffic to be handled. During the refurbishment of the South Western footbridge, the luggage lifts and segregated passageway were removed. In 1921, the carriage sidings required 185 staff, mostly shunters and cleaners, including two who operated the vacuum cleaning machines, and also a young lad who was responsible for labelling trains. Today, activity in the sidings is much reduced, with their role now mainly limited to off-peak stabling.

Above:

Unit No 508.002 stands in platform 10 with the 10.40 Shepperton to Waterloo train on 27 November 1982. On a wet morning, passengers on platform 10 emerge from the shelter of the awning in order to reach the subway, while a strip of damp paving emphasises the inadequacy of the cover over platform 11.
Ian Allan Library — Alex Dasi-Sutton

Most of the 27.75 acres of railway land at Clapham Junction is occupied by the South Western's sidings, with much of it no longer being fully utilised. At the northern extremity of the station, the former Kensington sidings, once the focus of milk and parcel traffic activity, are now reduced to four engineer's sidings which see little use. On the other side of the Windsor Line are nine long electrified sidings, one of which extends some distance towards Wandsworth Town and usually contains a long line of Class 455 units. Next are six non-electrified roads with an engine release crossover, used to stable West of England loco-hauled stock; during the middle of the day two formations each headed by a Class 50 could often be found here. In the centre of the yard, between platforms 6 and 7, two stacks of portacabins have replaced the accommodation block built in 1956 to house the then numerous yard staff and train crews.

Additional non-electrified sidings which led into the old carriage repair shed are now used mainly by engineer's trains awaiting weekend work. After withdrawal from service, one of the PEP units lingered here for several years. Then follow more electrified sidings in the open next to the SR-built car shed with

its six roads (four now electrified). Finally there is the area of the former milk docks and sidings below the Granada cinema. Here can be found any spare locos, usually of Classes 33, 47 or 73, as well as odd vehicles of all kinds, often including the crew training saloon which, attached to a Class 33 or 73 loco, follows a programme of rail tours to impart route knowledge to drivers and guards under instruction.

Clapham Yard is now mainly used to stable stock between the morning and evening peak periods within easy reach of Waterloo. In 1990, some 21 trains entered the yard during the latter part of the morning, passing through the carriage washing plant en route, and after internal cleaning and any necessary attention, 17 trains left the sidings ready for the evening rush hour. There was another influx of trains

during the late evening and about a dozen stabled overnight departing early the following morning. Altogether the yard handled 87 arrivals and departures on a normal Monday to Friday, all empty trains to and from Waterloo being Driver-Only Operated (DOO).

Wimbledon Park yard houses the remainder of Waterloo's peak-hour electric stock during the midday quiet period; in 1990, 14 trains arrived via East Putney after the morning rush hour and 17 returned to Waterloo in the afternoon, necessarily via the main line. Outside peak periods it is possible to work empty trains into Wimbledon Park sidings off the main line at Durnsford Road.

The renovation of Clapham Junction station during the 1980s included the repair and reglazing of

Right:
**No 73125 leaves Clapham Yard on
3 October 1974 with saloon
No DM395280 at the start of a route
knowledge tour for trainee guards.**
Ian Allan Library — J.Scrace

awnings, the cleaning and repainting of platform buildings and the retiling of the subway and its stairways. Other improvements could still be made if finance became available — perhaps from disposal of the surplus land around the sidings? Shelter and amenities for passengers are inadequate on the busy South Western platforms 9,10 and 11; the Central footbridge needs renewal, preferably in a style matching its South Western continuation; while wider and better stairways to platforms 7 to 15 are required. In the days of semaphore signalling, a mechanical indicator on the Central footbridge (probably worked by the booking lad in 'C' box) told passengers whether the next train to Victoria would leave from platform 12 or platform 14. In this era of information technology, a small group of customers is always gathered on the footbridge between these platforms waiting to see for themselves whether a main line train arrives at platform 12 before a local leaves from 14.

During the 1970s the Central main line platforms 12 and 13 were successively lengthened at the Victoria end to accommodate 12-car trains. Now that the South Western side is also being served by long distance trains, its up fast platforms 7 and 8 are restricted in length by St John's Hill bridge, which causes problems with the opening of the power-operated doors at the rear of a two-unit train of Class 442 stock. The West London platforms 16 and 17 were built for local traffic only, and are too short for the InterCity trains now calling at Clapham Junction — with a southbound train, nearly half of the usual eight coaches are off platform 17.

Moving to the freight scene, in the 1990-91 timetable there were only three or four freight trains in each direction between the West London line and the Central sector. These included two last survivors: a Speedlink working from Willesden to Crawley; and one of the few trains still carrying domestic coal, a twice-weekly trip from Didcot to Hove worked by a Class 37 loco. Occasional oil tank trains ran as required to different destinations, but the most important traffic was the daily Foster Yeoman stone train from Merehead Quarry to Crawley, worked by one of the company's Class 59 locos. The Class 59/1 locos of Foster Yeoman's rivals ARC can also now be

seen at Clapham Junction on trains from Whatley Quarry to Ardingly.

On the South Western side, Clapham Yard itself saw unaccustomed freight traffic while the junctions at Wimbledon were inoperative; the stone trains between Tolworth and Whatley Quarry had to reverse in the sidings, while the empty aggregate train from Tolworth to Newhaven had to traverse the yard to reach the Longhedge line. The Windsor Line carries more traffic, most of it to and from Kent via Longhedge and Factory Junctions; these include cement trains from the Thamesside works bound for a variety of distribution depots, MGR trains from the Midlands bringing coal for the cement industry (usually hauled by Class 56 diesels), aggregate traffic from Angerstein Wharf, and a short-term movement of contaminated soil from Chatham Dockyard to a landfill site on the Bedford-Bletchley line. Altogether nine or 10 trains daily would pass through in each direction; sometimes one would be recessed into the yard to await a change of locomotive or train crew. Besides these freight workings, the Windsor side occasionally sees a diesel loco arriving off the West London line hauling an ac electric unit bound for overhaul at Eastleigh works.

Freight traffic via the WLER 'main line' was heavier with over a score of trains in each direction passing Latchmere Junction in 1990-91. In addition to those bound for the Central lines at Clapham Junction, which have already been mentioned, there were Speedlink services to and from the Dover train ferry and Sheerness steelworks, freightliners from the new Isle of Grain terminal, and oil tank trains from Ripple Lane yard to various distribution points — all usually worked by the ubiquitous Class 47 locos. Aggregate business included a short distance transit across London from Angerstein Wharf to Park Royal or Westbourne Park hauled by pairs of Class 33 diesels. The same couplage worked Yeomans or Brett Marine stone trains from the Isle of Grain to Crawley yard via the old Longhedge Junction to Pouparts Junction route, storming through Clapham Junction station on the fast lines. The major traffic of Mendip stone into Kent used to be worked by Class 56 locos, but ARC now employs its own General Motors diesels of Class 59/1 on trains from Whatley Quarry. These company trains are liable to frequent change as dictated by supply contracts and the state of the construction industry, so by the time these words are in print a different pattern of operation may have evolved.

Wherever individual trains may go, the West London line is unlikely to recover its former activity, and the capacity will exist to run an all-day passenger service from Clapham Junction to Kensington and Willesden Junction. Before its demise the Greater London Council investigated this possibility and estimated its cost in 1983 at £3.5 million, including the provision of five or six intermediate stations. Electrification of the West London line will now be taking place as part of the Channel Tunnel project, and the only additional sections at Clapham Junction to be equipped for a local service would be the short links from Latchmere Junction into platform 2 and as far as the Pig Hill crossover outside platforms 16 and 17. BR considers that the service would not be profitable and that the cost of the new stations would have to be funded by the local authorities.

The Channel Tunnel will itself bring much additional traffic to the West London line, and therefore its track is being renewed to full main line standard. The Chelsea railway bridge has required major repairs and strengthening. During the 1950s, under WR control, all its steam classes except the 'Kings' and the '28xx' 2-8-0s were allowed over it (the LMR '8F' 2-8-0s were passed, however). Subsequently, severe speed restrictions were imposed, and for a period only one train at a time was allowed on the bridge. Despite re-decking in 1969, a complete reconstruction of the superstructure began in 1990 with single line working in force on weekdays and full occupation on Sundays with the InterCity trains being diverted via Guildford and Redhill. The West London line will also be resignalled all the way from Latchmere Junction to Willesden Junction, displacing some of the last semaphore signals in London at Kensington Olympia. The new colour light signals will be controlled from the Clapham Junction signalling centre, where modern SSI technology is expected to be used for the extended area, in contrast to the existing panels with which it will be linked.

The direct passenger trains via the Tunnel to the North of England as well as much of the through freight traffic will reach the West London via Factory Junction and Longhedge Junction; it has been proposed to reverse some of the rationalisation carried out in 1978-79 and restore the two independent pairs of tracks by abolishing Culvert Road Junction. However, the connection from the Chatham main line at Factory Junction to the West London at Latchmere Junction will never be a high-speed route. It is not expected at present that the through trains to and from the Midlands and North will call at Kensington Olympia for passenger traffic. Stops may be made, however, to pick up or set down Customs & Immigration officers, but any major development of Olympia station now appears unlikely.

Half of the freight traffic to and from the Tunnel is expected to run via Redhill, thus it will pass through Clapham Junction station en route to the West London line. Probably, most of the international freight trains will run at night when passenger and shuttle traffic through the Tunnel will be lighter, and this will reduce the difficulty of finding paths within the busy Central suburban area. Unfortunately the layout at Clapham Junction is less than ideal; the various widenings of the LBSCR main line have pushed the West London tracks into a succession of sharp reverse curves through the platforms, at the top of the

steep rise from the bridge under the lines to Waterloo and Victoria. Memories remain of an 'N' class 2-6-0 stalling here on an Inter-Regional holiday express and having to await banking assistance from a 'W' class tank; even diesels had their troubles, a Class 25 once taking 15 minutes to restart a freight from platform 17, slipping furiously all the time. Hopefully the power of the Class 92 electric locos will make light of this climb.

The reverse curves through platforms 16 and 17 and the sharp turnout from the Central slow lines (where derailments have taken place) enforce an overall 20mph speed limit for West London trains. This could be eased, and these platforms lengthened, by extending the St John's Hill bridge and widening the cutting beyond. Although the Masonic Girls' School has long since moved, its site is occupied by a Peabody Trust block of flats, and to encroach on this land would probably be financially and politically impracticable. Thus Clapham Junction seems set to become one of the crawling points on the journey to and from the Channel Tunnel.

The most interesting development in connection with the Channel Tunnel will be the reopening of the spur from Latchmere Junction to West London Junction, now referred to as Sheepcote Lane Junction. This is being done primarily to allow the TMST trains from Waterloo to reach their maintenance depot at North Pole Junction, Old Oak Common. However, this connection will also be used by some passenger services; initially, until the divisible North of England version of the TMST units is available, substitute trains (probably HSTs) will run from the Midlands and North into Waterloo International to make cross-platform interchange with services to Paris and Brussels. In the longer term there may be similar connections from South Wales and the West of England, where the absence of electrification makes international through services impossible.

This reopened connection is an example of how the Channel Tunnel development has impinged on the Waterloo Area Resignalling Scheme. Conceived in the days of panel diagrams and relay rooms, it has been overtaken by the era of the VDU and solid state electronics. The TMST high speed trains will be equipped with the latest and most sophisticated forms of on-board signalling, but will have to share tracks with traditional 1960s vintage SR EMUs. The modest changes to the existing layout originally planned have had to be revised to provide for the huge new International terminal with extensive track alterations between Waterloo and Clapham Junction. Added to the trauma of the Clapham Junction disaster, it is not surprising that completion of the major part of the WARS scheme at Easter 1991 was some two years later than initially estimated.

The new Wimbledon signalling centre should provide much-needed flexibility in handling domestic traffic in and out of Waterloo, which has lost the use

Above:
Eastleigh works carries out overhauls and refurbishment on other regions' electric stock. Here No 37089 arrives at Clapham Junction with ac unit No 302.304 on 30 March 1983. A Class 73 electro-diesel will take over for the journey to Eastleigh. *Author*

Below:
The Windsor Line through Clapham Junction sees a regular flow of MGR coal trains from the Midlands to the Kentish cement works and paper mills. A return empty train passes beneath 'A' box on 4 September 1986, double-headed by Nos 73121 and 73102, before these became dedicated InterCity Class 73/2 locos. *Ian Allan Library — Chris Wilson*

Top:
Stone and aggregate traffic is liable to frequent change: for a time Foster Yeoman operated a train between the Isle of Grain and Crawley, and the return empties are seen here from Freemasons Bridge on 13 April 1989, worked by Nos 33202 and 33063. The train is running on the up fast line so as to be able to diverge at Pouparts Junction towards Longhedge Junction. *C.J.Marsden*

Above:
Domestic coal business was obviously light as the last surviving working, the empty Hove to Didcot train, passes New Wandsworth on 13 April 1989, hauled by No 37131. *C.J.Marsden*

Above:
No 59002 *Yeoman Enterprise* winds the wagons of the Crawley to Merehead empties through platform 16 on 1 September 1990. *Alex Dasi-Sutton*

of two of its platforms and one of its approach tracks as part of the International project. At one stage it was proposed to divert some of the Windsor Line suburban trains into Victoria via Longhedge Junction and Stewarts Lane, which would also have served 'The Battersea' leisure centre proposed for the site of the old power station — a scheme which remains in limbo. The end of mail and parcels traffic, the drop in inner suburban business and the cessation of loco-haulage at Waterloo may enable the terminus to cope with these reduced facilities.

Of the trains passing through Clapham Junction, some 95% are electric, but diesel traction is not likely to disappear completely. Certainly, electrification of the West London line for Channel Tunnel traffic will eliminate the diesel-worked 'Kenny Belle'. It is also probable that the third rail will eventually be extended to Uckfield, bringing to an end the last three DEMU workings out of Victoria. However the decision to replace loco-hauled trains on the Waterloo-Exeter line by Class 159 Express DMUs rather than by electrification will retain diesel traction at Waterloo for the foreseeable future. If InterCity cross-country trains off the former Western Region to Gatwick and Brighton continue to run, they will remain diesel-worked, although the through train to Kent is not likely to survive the opening of the Channel Tunnel. While international freight will be electrically worked, most domestic MGR, bulk and company

trains will continue to be diesel-hauled. With the coming of the latest generation of electric trains — the '319', '455' and '456' classes — Clapham Junction will not see the future 'Networker' era for many years.

Recession in 1990-91 brought about a downturn in commuter and off-peak travel within Network South-East, and many investment projects have been pigeon-holed. If daily journeys in and out of Central London are now declining from the boom levels of the late 1980s, there is a growing demand for rail links which will cater for orbital travel between suburban centres. Local authorities have sponsored investigations into the possibilities of adapting parts of the South London network into either some form of light railway, with street-running extensions, or into an improved heavy rail system with new connections to facilitate frequent orbital services. It is not yet clear to what extent these new routes would replace the traditional services to and from the London termini which make up so much of the activity at Clapham Junction. Interchange at the junction may take new forms in the next century.

Select Bibliography

The London & South Western Railway: (2 Vols)
   R.A.Williams
The LSWR in the Twentieth Century: J.N.Faulkner &
   R.A.Williams
The South Western Railway: C.Hamilton Ellis
The London Brighton & South Coast Railway (3 Vols):
   J.T.Howard Turner
London Brighton & South Coast Railway: C.Hamilton
   Ellis
The London Chatham & Dover Railway: Adrian Gray
History of the Southern Railway: C.Dendy Marshall
   (Ian Allan Ltd)
Sir Herbert Walker's Southern Railway: C.F.Klapper
History of the Southern Railway: M.R.Bonavia
Southern Region Chronology & Record: R.H.Clark
Southern Electric: G.T.Moody (Ian Allan Ltd)
West London Railway: H.V.Borley & R.W.Kidner
West London Joint Railways: J.B.Atkinson (Ian Allan
   Ltd)
*Locomotive Histories of the LSWR, LBSCR, SECR and
   SR:* published by the RCTS

The 'Bournemouth Belle' passed away with the steam era.
Three months before the end, Standard Class 4 2-6-4T
No 80133 leaves Clapham Yard for Waterloo with the empty
stock on 8 April 1967. *Ian Allan Library — John H. Bird*